10/12

Railroads
of
COLORADO

Your Guide to
Colorado's Historic Trains
and Railway Sites

Claude Wiatrowski

FARCOUNTRY
PRESS

HELENA, MONTANA

IN MEMORY OF MY MOTHER, EMILIE,
WHO INSPIRED ME TO DO GREAT THINGS.

Page 1: *A westbound train carefully creeps onto Lobato Trestle, the second highest on the Cumbres & Toltec Scenic Railroad.*

Page 2-3: *An authentic Rio Grande narrow-gauge train stands guard on a trestle in the Black Canyon, just east of the Cimarron Visitor Center.*

Page 3 inset: *Now retired at the Colorado Railroad Museum, this Rio Grande stock car once carried livestock through the Colorado mountains.*

Facing page: *The author's children, Karen and Kevin, ride a caboose at the Colorado Railroad Museum.*

Page 6: *One of the largest narrow-gauge locomotives once used by the Rio Grande sees service today on the Durango & Silverton.*

ISBN 10: 1-56037-529-9
ISBN 13: 978-1-56037-529-6

© 2012 by Farcountry Press
Text and Photographs © 2002 by the Mountain Automation Corporation

For more information, write Farcountry Press, P.O. Box 5630, Helena, MT 59604; call (800) 821-3874; or visit www.farcountrypress.com.

Cataloging-in-Publication Data is on file at the Library of Congress.

Printed in China.

15   14   13   12   1   2   3   4   5   6   7

ACKNOWLEDGMENTS

This book would not have been written without my wife, Margaret. She understands my love of Colorado railroad history. For decades, she hiked abandoned mountain railroad pathways, rode preserved railroads, and drove the car as I searched for one more place to take yet one more photograph.

I am sure that my children, Kevin and Karen, thought that everyone frequently rode steam trains. Waiting to board a modern Amtrak passenger train in La Junta, Colorado, a very young Kevin asked me, "Dad, where are the Santa Fe's steam engines?" I had to tell him that it had been decades since the Santa Fe used steam engines. Both of them know about coal tipples, roundhouses, turntables, and water tanks—terms quite foreign to their peers. They provided years of pleasant company for their dad on railroad excursions.

At the very real risk of missing someone, many people have helped me with this book or just helped me enjoy exploring Colorado's railroads over the years. These include Martin and Ursula Frick, Doug Doane, Spencer Wren, Zola Lyons, Patty Amend, Myrna Ellinger, Bob Richardson, Charles Albi, William Gould, Kenton Forrest, Lindsey and Rosa Ashby, Dan and Karen Ranger, Bill Lock, Spencer Wilson, Amos Cordova, Jeffrey Jackson, Kristi Nelson Cohen, Rich Millard, Ken and Stephanie Olsen, Jim and Liz Birmingham, Hugo and Elizabeth Lackman, Deborah Van Broekhoven, Brooke and Karolyn Smith, Bill and Barb McKenzie, Al Dunton, Mel McFarland, Roger Smith, James Stitzel, Ed and Nancy Bathke, Evan Ammeson, and Margret Aldrich.

I'd especially like to thank all the employees of the Manitou & Pike's Peak Railway who have given me so much enjoyment over a quarter century, as well as the members of the Colorado Midland Chapter of the National Railway Historical Society whose lectures and field trips introduced me to many of Colorado's railroad treasures.

Finally, none of Colorado's railroad history would be here today without the foresighted individuals and organizations that preserved it. Railroad employees and volunteers make Colorado's history come alive at operating railroads and museums throughout the state.

CONTENTS

PREFACE

Many books have been written about Colorado's railroads and more are published every year. Necessarily, they delve into increasingly detailed descriptions of railroad history and technology. For readers new to Colorado's railroad history, these details tend to obscure why Colorado's historic railroads are so exciting. Even photo essays on these mountain treasures are usually targeted at readers that already understand their special nature.

Although you'll find history in these pages, this is also an inspirational book—a book for you to enjoy—a book to convince you that the railroads of Colorado are special and worthy of further exploration, in print and in person. You'll be inspired to read more about the bygone days of Colorado's railroads, to hike the abandoned railroad grades threaded through its mountains, and to experience the preserved railways that still challenge its granite peaks. You need not be a dedicated railroad enthusiast or an academic historian to enjoy the stories of Colorado's railroad history.

What makes Colorado's mountain railroads so inspirational? One answer is that Colorado's trains chugged through beautiful mountain settings and climbed to the edge of the sky, but there are many more characteristics that interact to inspire devotion among those who truly understand their story. Located in extreme places, they are tributes to the ingenuity of the engineers that designed them. They went everywhere in the mountains. Frequently served by more than one railroad, sleepy agricultural hamlets and pretentious mining towns offered public rail transportation to the rest of the country. As well as transporting people and daily necessities, these trains carried everything from gold, silver, and marble to coal, livestock, and lumber. Colorado's railroads were built with an optimism not justified by the available traffic, and most were doomed from the day their first spike was driven—but everyone loves an underdog.

Colorado's mountains sheltered all kinds of railroads. Giant steam locomotives lumbered up river valleys and tiny narrow-gauge engines traversed the most precipitous mountain gateways. Electric railroads silently floated down mountainsides. Trolleys carried miners from homes to headframes. With little traffic and no incentive to rebuild old tracks, ancient train operations survived well into the twentieth century. Lasting into the 1940s and 1950s, many miles of track guided trains that had already become museum-quality relics. Amazingly, narrow-gauge steam-powered freight trains ran until 1968. Because Colorado's historic trains survived so long, much antique railroad equipment and even entire sections of operating railroads were preserved to be enjoyed today.

Many characteristics, such as breathtaking scenery, flow through this entire book. *Railroads of Colorado* is, however, divided into parts, each part emphasizing railroads with a common trait—although all Colorado's mountain railroads shared most of the attributes that made them so special.

Each chapter includes a short guide on exploring the railroads described therein. Inquire locally for specific directions and information about driving or hiking old railroad grades. Depending on current conditions, unpaved roads may be closed or impassable, especially to low-ground-clearance vehicles. Hiking may be inadvisable in bad weather. Respect the fact that railroads are private property. Ask first! Some antique railroad structures are preserved by volunteers. Others are deteriorating in the icy snows. Please take care of all of these relics so your grandchildren as well as mine will be able to enjoy them.

Facing page: About a third of the Manitou & Pike's Peak Railway route is host to the lavish autumn colors of the Rockies.

Inset: A Durango & Silverton train waits for its passengers to finish exploring Silverton.

A MAGICAL PLACE

In 1971, my wife, Margaret, and I were determined to explore at least some of the Four Corners region of Colorado, Utah, Arizona, and New Mexico. We were graduate students at the University of Arizona and hadn't had the time or money to explore more than Tucson, where we went to school. We could reasonably expect to move somewhere else in the country for employment and wanted to experience the West before we left.

I had heard there was a narrow-gauge steam train in Durango, Colorado. Like most young boys of the 1950s, I had been infatuated with trains, so I wanted to see this one. We arrived too late in the day to ride it, but a railroad employee suggested we make the three-hour drive to Chama, New Mexico, to see its railroad facilities. I had never heard of Chama, but our railroad friend was very insistent. Since we had nothing planned for the rest of the day, Margaret and I headed east toward Chama.

We found a quiet, charming small town, a vision right out of the Old West. Guessing the direction of the railroad yards, we quickly crossed narrow-gauge tracks bordered by a stock pen. How long must it have been since livestock were carried in these narrow-gauge trains? I could only imagine, and wondered why the pens were still intact. Soon we could see diminutive railroad cars lined up through the trees—wooden cars from the last century—a sea of little cars.

Most remnants of the steam-locomotive era had disappeared from Chicago by the time I was growing up there. Besides, my parents were not in the habit of frequenting railroad yards. But on this clear, spring day, all those miniatures I had seen in *Model Railroader* magazine were here, almost full size and standing right in front of me. I had never seen trains this small. Their tiny size gave this place a charm I did not expect from a railroad yard. We drifted through the area not believing our eyes. There was a water tank to quench the thirst of steam locomotives and a coal tipple to deliver the food they burned in their bellies. Two stalls of a roundhouse, once host to sizzling iron horses, stood silently. Steam locomotives littered the area. There were two rotary snowplows, giant steam-powered snow blowers, a pile driver, other odd equipment I did not recognize, and what seemed like hundreds of tiny freight cars. We were window-shopping in a huge model train store except everything was real.

With the street and its modern automobiles out of sight, you couldn't tell if it was 1940, 1920, or 1900. I later learned that we were witness to both a birth and a death. The last narrow-gauge steam-powered freight trains had chugged through Chama about three years earlier. This century-old railroad yard and the sixty-plus miles of track east over the mountains to Antonito, Colorado, had just been saved by the state governments of Colorado and New Mexico. Unfortunately, much of the narrow gauge had also just been lost—the mainline to Durango and Farmington, the repair shops at Alamosa, a huge cache of historic

Facing page: Narrow-gauge track strikes out south from Silverton through the canyon of the Animas River.

Inset: Crewmembers of the Cumbres & Toltec lean into the curve at Los Pinos loop.

railroad equipment—everything except the railroads from Chama to Antonito and Durango to Silverton.

The steam locos at Chama were silent. Not a rusty wheel turned. On that May day in 1971, we traveled back to Durango to watch the train from Silverton arrive. Not until later would I learn that the railroad from Chama to Antonito came back to life in that summer of 1971. Its little passenger trains would struggle uphill just a few times that year.

After a night near Durango, we drove northward over the most rugged mountains we had ever seen. Arizona had mountains, but nothing like Colorado's San Juans. We dropped into Silverton—and the correct word is dropped. Silverton sits in a dimple in the San Juan Mountains, a small mountain valley called Bakers Park. Here we caught up with the other end of the track from Durango. It had been hiding in the Animas River canyon. With a name like Silverton, it was easy to guess what the mines produced and why a railroad was built to this place. How tough were the men that discovered these silver mines, that built this railroad, that lived and worked in what seemed like the end of the earth? Although steam trains still

chugged into town, we soon discovered they once went even farther. Incredibly, we drove higher up an old railroad grade to the ghost town of Animas Forks. We passed a silver mill and other evidences of human endeavors. Essentially running a railroad entirely above timberline, the men that pushed trains this high must have indeed been made of steel. As we drove higher, snow still covered the ground, even in spring. I wondered how they ran trains in the winter and later found out they didn't.

We headed east. Passing through Sargents on our climb up Monarch Pass, I spotted another railroad water tank. Railroad buildings nestled in this mountain valley as well. Our Colorado Springs visit included a brief stop at the cog railroad up Pikes Peak. I had seen Pikes Peak once before, and you couldn't have convinced me that anyone could build a railroad to its top. Yet here it was—a funny railroad with teeth down the center of its track that allowed it to climb the awesome mountain. We didn't have enough time to ride this train either. By now, I knew I had made a scheduling blunder and resolved to return to ride all these incredible trains.

"Soon we could see diminutive railroad cars lined up through the trees—wooden cars from the last century—a sea of little cars."

RAILROAD TECHNOLOGY

Railroads revolutionized society when steam locomotives were invented to power long, heavy trains of cars at high speeds. Steam locomotives burn fuel to boil water to make steam. Fuel and water are usually carried in a tender, a railroad car pulled behind the engine. The steam produced is used to drive a piston back and forth to move the wheels of the locomotive.

Raised cylindrical wooden water tanks lined Colorado's railroad tracks during the heyday of the steam locomotive. When possible, water was diverted from streams higher up on the mountain to the tanks, allowing gravity to keep them full. Gravity also allowed huge amounts of water to flow from these tanks into the locomotive tenders. Steam locomotives can be fueled by anything that will burn. In Colorado, this almost always meant coal. The black fuel

was usually lifted mechanically into a bin, or coal tipple, from which it could be dropped, again aided by gravity, to quickly fill a locomotive's tender.

In the United States, railroad track usually consists of two steel rails spiked to wooden crossties. These ties keep the rails the correct distance apart as well as transfer the weight of the train to the ground beneath the track. Ballast is the rock packed around the ties to keep them from shifting and to allow water to drain without washing away the earth under the rails. A switch is an arrangement of track that allows trains to follow different routes. A mechanical lever on a switchstand selects one route or the other.

Daily locomotive maintenance was performed in structures called enginehouses, and one was erected virtually everywhere locos had to

wait for their next assignments. In large railroad centers, the arrangement of track and switches connecting many enginehouse stalls would be unreasonably long. Instead, a turntable—a bridge-like structure in a circular pit—was used to move the locomotives to different tracks. A locomotive would pull onto the turntable, which was spun around to align the locomotive with the desired track. An enginehouse built in a circular shape surrounding a turntable is called a roundhouse.

Steam locomotives run better forward than backward. Thus, they must be turned for return trips. Turntables were also used for this purpose, although they were quite expensive. A triangular arrangement of track, called a wye, was more common. Less frequently, a loop of track would allow the locomotive to circle around and change direction.

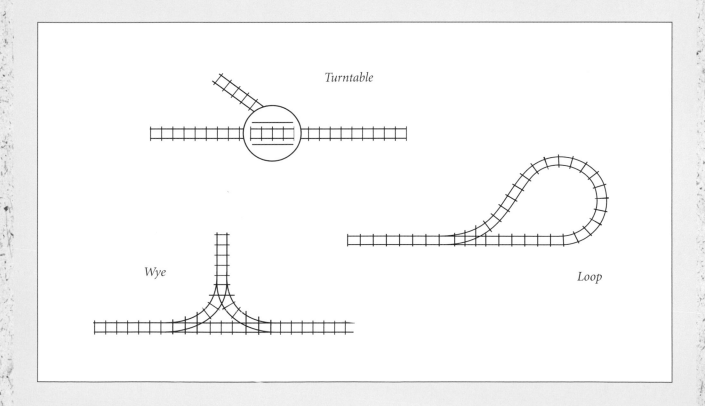

Turntable

Loop

Wye

How Trains Climb

When a railroad must climb, the preferred route is most often a water-level route, one that follows a river but only if that river's course is not too steep. Where the route of a river or creek rises too steeply to allow a railroad to follow alongside, the railroad is lengthened by looping its track through side canyons. Since the rails travel a longer distance to gain the same elevation, the track rises less steeply than does the river's course.

There may be no waterway where the railroad must go. In that case, the tracks run back and forth across a hillside in giant "steps" with loops of track connecting one step with the next. If there is no room for loops, the stair-steps of track are connected with switchbacks. These require the train to move forward up one track, a track switch to be thrown behind the train to change its route, and the train to move backward up the next rung of the ladder. This very time-consuming process is avoided at all costs, and switchbacks are seldom used today.

More extreme methods of climbing include the construction of a

The 14,110-foot summit of Pikes Peak rises over the newest train model of the Manitou & Pike's Peak on a sunny autumn day. These trains were built in Switzerland.

spiral track loop. The track actually crosses over itself after climbing to a higher elevation around the loop. When all else fails, a specialized technology may be employed. Cog railroads use a toothed rail down the center of the track to climb more steeply. Where grades are too steep even for a cog railroad, an incline railway uses a cable to haul railcars up the hill. All these extreme technologies found uses in Colorado's mountains.

The steepness of a railroad is measured in percent. A railroad that rises four feet while it moves forward one hundred feet is said to have a gradient of 4 percent. "Gradient" is often just shortened to "grade," a word also used to describe the roadbed on which the track rests. Steep grades increase energy costs, decrease train speeds, and make stopping difficult when going downhill. Today, grades as high as 4 percent are almost non-existent in the United States, although 4 percent grades were once very common in Colorado.

What's in a Name?

Railroad names are a difficult and confusing subject. Different portions of the same railroad may have had different corporate names. The consequences of a railroad bankruptcy, an all-too-frequent occurrence, resulted in a name change. Railroads merged with each other, also causing the line's name to be changed. Sometimes, names simply disappeared. A new name could be as subtle as changing *Railroad* to *Rail-way*. Locals had common names for Colorado's railroads that remained constant over the years. This book and the map that appears on pages 16-17 typically use these common names in an attempt to minimize confusion.

Railroads continued to change names after the time period covered in this book. The Denver & Rio Grande Western Railroad changed to the Southern Pacific Railroad and finally to the Union Pacific Railroad. The Colorado & Southern Railway became part of the Burlington Railroad, which became the Burlington Northern Railroad, which merged with the Santa Fe Railway to become the BNSF. The older names are indicated on the following map, which is a composite useful for following the text and for exploring the state's historic railroads.

Above: Rio Grande Southern locomotive 20, now at the Colorado Railroad Museum, may have once pulled these very freight cars over Lizard Head Pass.

Top: Several private cars, including the Alamosa, can be chartered on the Durango & Silverton.

By the time we left the Colorado Railroad Museum in Golden, I was hooked. We examined all of the railroad equipment on display, examined each historical photo, and read every word of every exhibit. Where was this elephant pushing a narrow-gauge train? What was this railroad zigzagging its way to a tunnel over eleven thousand feet above sea level? Why would anyone build a railroad to the very top of a mountain? We were going to have to come back.

Not only did we come back, we made Colorado our home. We've been exploring its ghost railways and riding its preserved trains ever since. In this book, I hope to convince you that Colorado is a magical place—a place where you can experience western history like nowhere else. Come to Colorado both to see the majestic places where iron horses once struggled and to ride historic trains that still climb through these mountains. You won't make the mistake I made on my first trip. You'll be sure you have time to ride all of Colorado's mountain railroads.

RAILROADS OF COLORADO

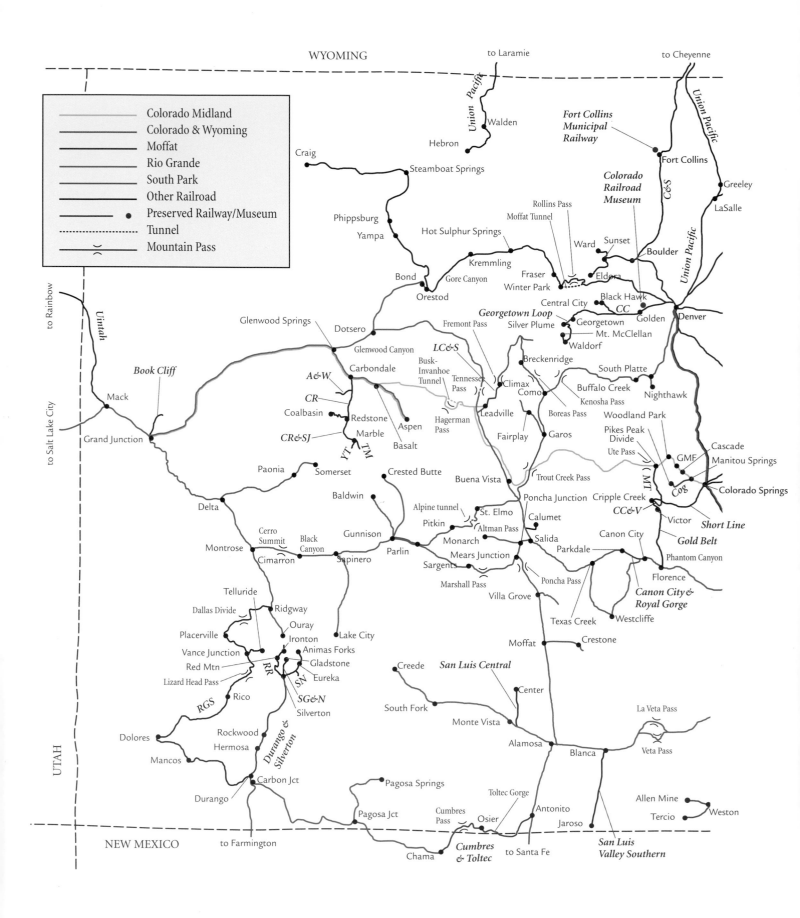

Legend:
- Colorado Midland
- Colorado & Wyoming
- Moffat
- Rio Grande
- South Park
- Other Railroad
- ● Preserved Railway/Museum
- Tunnel
- Mountain Pass

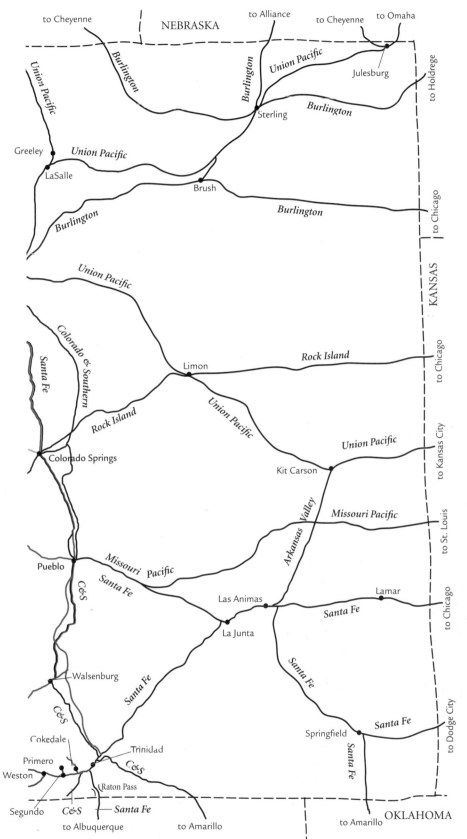

to Cheyenne NEBRASKA to Alliance to Cheyenne to Omaha

Burlington

Union Pacific

Burlington

Julesburg

to Holdrege

Union Pacific

Burlington

Burlington

Sterling

Burlington

Greeley

Union Pacific

LaSalle

Brush

Burlington

Burlington

to Chicago

KANSAS

Union Pacific

Colorado & Southern

Santa Fe

Union Pacific

Limon

Rock Island

to Chicago

Rock Island

Union Pacific

Colorado Springs

Union Pacific

to Kansas City

Kit Carson

Arkansas Valley

Missouri Pacific

to St. Louis

Pueblo

Missouri Pacific

C&S

Santa Fe

Las Animas

Lamar

Santa Fe

to Chicago

La Junta

Santa Fe

Walsenburg

Santa Fe

Santa Fe

to Dodge City

C&S

Cokedale

Trinidad

Springfield

Santa Fe

Primero

C&S

Santa Fe

Weston

Raton Pass

SG&N

Segundo C&S Santa Fe

OKLAHOMA

to Albuquerque to Amarillo to Amarillo

NOTES

• This map is a composite representing no single era in Colorado's history.
• Railroads shown are both existing track and abandoned grade.
• Multiple railroads on the same alignment are shown as a single line.
• Railroads not shown include some north of Denver; many east of the mountains; coal-hauling railroads near Florence, Walsenburg, and Trinidad; and logging railroads near Pagosa Springs and Dolores.

ABBREVIATIONS

AC	Argentine Central
A&W	Aspen & Western
CC	Colorado Central
C&N	Colorado & Northwestern
C&S	Colorado & Southern
C&W	Colorado & Wyoming
CM	Colorado Midland
CC&V	Cripple Creek & Victor
CR	Crystal River
CR&SJ	Crystal River & San Juan
LC&S	Leadville, Colorado & Southern
MT	Midland Terminal
RGS	Rio Grande Southern
RR	Rainbow Route
SG&N	Silverton, Gladstone & Northerly
SN	Silverton Northern
TM	Treasury Mountain
YT	Yule Tram

PART I

TRAINS WITHOUT A PRAYER

Railroads were the most important technology of the nineteenth century and stoked the economic engines of the world. Much like modern-day Internet companies, however, they evoked irrational exuberance as railroad fever swept the United States. Colorado businessmen desperately wanted to compete with the rest of the country, and that meant building railroads into the mountains. Often, such lines were partly or completely justified by a recent gold or silver strike. Some of Colorado's railroads were touted as links in the great transcontinental railway web of the time. Thus, the words "and Pacific" were common embellishments to a Colorado railroad's corporate name, although neither the Denver, South Park & Pacific Railroad nor the Denver, Northwestern & Pacific Railway ever came close to smelling the salt air of their namesake ocean.

Colorado's mountain railroads didn't have a ghost of a chance. Too many trains traveled to too many places with no chance of recovering the investment of constructing the railroad. Many lines did not even generate enough revenue to profitably operate trains, let alone pay back investors. Sufficient passenger and freight traffic simply didn't exist in the small, remote towns to which these railroads were built. Some doomed railroads did find adequate business initially, but that business disappeared when a natural resource played out or the market price for a commodity hauled by the railroad sank. Sometimes, traffic disappeared even before the railroad reached its destination.

Amid all this misfortune, a railway was constructed from the financial wreckage of several smaller lines. This section describes two railroads that became part of the Colorado & Southern, a company created from the merger of bankrupt railroads.

This Georgetown Loop locomotive will take the curving track to the left and soon cross the Devil's Gate Bridge.

CHAPTER 1

CHASING ITS TAIL

The Colorado Central Railroad

In 1861, William Loveland looked east from his office in Golden, Colorado, and could see the coming of the transcontinental railroad. Although it would be six years before railroad track even nicked the edge of Colorado, Loveland knew that cities on the new transcontinental route would prosper and those bypassed would wither away. Loveland looked west and saw only a small hole in the rampart of the Rocky Mountains, a canyon from which Clear Creek emptied. This *must* be a path to the Pacific. It was the only hope for Golden to thrive on a transcontinental rail route. If you've driven winding U.S. Highway 6 through this narrow, rocky canyon, you know the hope of a major transcontinental route through Colorado's rugged mountains was a faint hope indeed.

Loveland hired engineer Edward Berthoud to find this route to the western ocean. Berthoud and famed mountain man Jim Bridger rode west up Clear Creek. Imagine the enormity of the task to find a railroad route to the Pacific Ocean! Maps were primitive if they existed at all. There were no aerial photos or global positioning system satellites. Hearsay was the common method of navigation. Several months of exploration as far as Utah led Berthoud to propose a railroad that would crest just west of Golden. U.S. Highway 40 now tops this location, called Berthoud Pass, at over eleven thousand feet above sea level.

Swiss-born Berthoud had heard of the world's first narrow-gauge railroads in Wales and suggested that narrow-gauge track be used on the route from Golden to minimize the cost of construction. Federal law decreed the first transcontinental railroad was to be standard gauge, however, and as dreams of a transcontinental route still floated in the heads of the

Facing page: A Georgetown Loop passenger train creeps across Devil's Gate Bridge, just as Colorado Central trains once did.

Inset: Colorado & Southern loco 71 simmers softly near Central City. You can no longer ride the train here, a line once part of the Colorado Central.

On March 29, 1884, just before regular passenger service began to Silver Plume, the Colorado Central carefully staged this photo of four trains on the Georgetown Loop for William Henry Jackson's camera. The one-car train in the foreground was the photographer's special, carrying the chemicals and darkroom needed to prepare and develop the glass plate negative on which this image was captured. (Courtesy, Colorado Historical Society, WHJ-256. Photo by W. H. Jackson.)

good citizens of Golden, it was decided that narrow-gauge track would just not do.

General Grenville Dodge, chief engineer of the Union Pacific's transcontinental construction, joined Berthoud on an expedition into the mountains in 1866 to assess the possibility of a rail line through the Rockies. Assaulted by an early fall blizzard and precipitous terrain, Dodge was not impressed. He would build the transcontinental route through Wyoming. All of Colorado, including Golden, would be bypassed.

The Siren Song of Silver and Gold

In 1858, placer gold was discovered in streams near the present site of Denver, and prospectors were pulled into the mountains along the creeks, hoping to find the source of this gold. In 1859, gold was discovered at Idaho Springs, Central City, and Georgetown. The difficulty of transporting supplies and machinery to the mines, and ore from them, however, quickly put a ceiling on the wealth that could be generated in any of these locations.

Finally, in 1872, the Colorado Central Railroad began construction of a narrow-gauge railroad up Clear Creek from Golden. The Colorado Central, which stretched about fifty miles from Denver to its farthest extent a few miles west of Silver Plume, would be short compared to other Colorado mountain railroads. It also traversed no spectacular mountain passes, usually avoiding the snow-removal problems of railroads that did. Yet, the Colorado Central was the prototype of Colorado's mountain rail lines, challenging the peaks with narrow-gauge tracks and tapping the wealth created by wrenching precious metals from the ground. But like its sister railroads, it would ultimately prove unsuccessful for those who invested the substantial sums required for its construction.

Fueled by mining, the demand for transportation up Clear Creek was intense in the last half of the nineteenth century. Track was initially laid up the north fork of Clear Creek to Black Hawk in 1872. Completion of the line to Central City in 1878 required a four-mile struggle, including two switchbacks and a trestle that flew trains right over Black Hawk's main streets. Since it was only one and one-quarter miles to Central City by wagon, this additional construction was unlikely to be worth its cost, but it was the principle of the thing and the optimism that a railroad was always better!

Construction up the main fork of Clear Creek did not resume until 1877 when trains reached Georgetown. By 1864, the quality of the town's gold ore had declined to the point where it was not worth mining. In that same year, just in the nick of time, Georgetown was saved by the discovery of rich silver ore. Soon, it was the fastest growing city in Colorado. Homes, churches, commercial establishments, and public buildings grew like weeds, and many of these buildings still stand in Georgetown for you to enjoy.

The Far-Famed Loop

Many mines and mills lay near the town of Silver Plume, less than two miles southwest of Georgetown, but the area's narrow valley and almost seven-hundred-foot increase in elevation made the construction of a railroad impractical—or so it was thought.

Union Pacific civil engineer Jacob Blickensderfer was assigned the problem of locating this proposed railroad. Blickensderfer used the experience and knowledge of his sixty-three years to devise the ingenious solution of the "Georgetown Loop." Trains would circumnavigate a spiral track, crossing over their own route on the gargantuan Devil's Gate Bridge, which would be three hundred feet long and rise almost a hundred feet over Clear Creek, spanning a rocky notch near Georgetown. In addition to Dev-

THE WELSH CONNECTION

Initially, separating Colorado's silver metal from its ore was difficult, but technology from Wales installed in a Black Hawk smelter eventually proved successful. Wales provided Colorado not only with smelting technology but also with railroad technology. The distance between railroad rails is called the gauge. Railroads had been built with a standard gauge of 4 feet 8½ inches, or wider, until the first narrower track was built in Wales. Although a narrower gauge may seem like a trivial change, many did not believe railroads this narrow could be made to work. Welsh railroad track was only about two feet wide and demonstrated that narrow-gauge railroads could be profitably operated where wider-gauge tracks would be impossibly expensive to construct. Longer distances and heavier projected traffic led Colorado's pioneer railroad builders to space their rails three feet apart.

The world's prototype narrow-gauge railroad is the Festiniog Railway in Wales. Built as a horse-drawn tramway in 1836 to carry slate from the mountains to the sea, it received its first steam locomotive in 1863. It carries passengers today.

At Silver Plume, the Georgetown Loop's Shay locomotive 14 waits below a mountainside blanketed with nineteenth-century mines.

il's Gate Bridge, three hairpin turns and three smaller bridges were needed. Altogether, the track would curve the equivalent of three and one-half complete circles. Trains first arrived in Silver Plume over the Georgetown Loop in 1884. Little steam locomotives pulling a few cars would slowly creep up to Silver Plume, changing compass headings again and again.

Why would anyone build such a complex and expensive railroad just to travel the two miles to Silver Plume? By now, the Union Pacific controlled the Colorado Central, and the dream of a through railroad route along Clear Creek was not yet dead. The dream's original destination, the Pacific Ocean, had been replaced by nearby Leadville, where an outrageous silver strike had created a town of fourteen thousand, and mines spewed out more wealth than the Georgetown

miners could ever hope to extract. The railroad's extension from Georgetown was projected to continue from Silver Plume and tunnel under Loveland Pass, but the project was abandoned when another Union Pacific–controlled railroad, the Denver, South Park & Pacific, reached Leadville along with two competitors, the Denver & Rio Grande and the Colorado Midland Railway. Although the Colorado Central chugged a few miles beyond Silver Plume, it never burrowed through Loveland Pass, a task later accomplished with the building of Interstate 70's Eisenhower Tunnel.

The End is in Sight

By 1899, several bankrupt railways, including the Colorado Central, were combined into a railroad named the Colorado & Southern. Virtually all the traffic on the Colorado Central had been related to mining, and although no one knew it in 1899, that industry had begun a long, slow decline from which it would never recover.

The Georgetown Loop was hardly worth the original cost of its construction, but it did have an unexpected side effect. Adventurous tourists flocked to ride trains over this engineering marvel. Trains would stop on the Devil's Gate Bridge to let brave passengers walk out ahead for a group photo. Such photos even show foolhardy souls dangling their feet from the edge of the span. Special trains ran from Denver Union Station carrying sightseers from all over the world.

The end of the authentic Wild West and the beginning of its preservation collided on a July day in 1932. The Central City Opera House was reopened after being restored to its gold-rush grandeur. Elegant patrons were delivered to Black Hawk by the last narrow-gauge passenger excursion train to travel up Clear Creek. One wonders if any of the guests ventured to speculate on the need to preserve the railway as well.

Traffic and service on the Clear Creek lines steadily declined. Trains ran only three times a week and then only twice. By 1939, the Loop had been dismantled and the Devil's Gate Bridge sold for less than five hundred dollars to a mining company. Colorado's first mountain railroad was merely a memory in a

photo album by 1941. The steel trail built up Clear Creek with such hope for the future had been completely removed in less than seventy years.

A New Beginning is at Hand

In 1959, just twenty years after the Loop had been dismantled, the Colorado Historical Society looked into the mountains where William Loveland had once gazed and saw the valley between Georgetown and Silver Plume as the perfect place to build a passenger train line—the Georgetown Loop Railroad. The society would acquire the old mines, mills, and railroad grade and create a living museum of Colorado's mining history. It was not easy. When Interstate 70 was constructed, for example, the society fought to have it located high up the mountainside so the valley bot-

Left: A narrow-gauge diesel loco is unloaded at Silver Plume to provide additional power for the Georgetown Loop.

Below: Reconstruction of Devil's Gate Bridge began in 1983 and was completed in 1984. The three-hundred-foot-long bridge launches Georgetown Loop trains over Clear Creek— one hundred feet in the air. The completed railway was officially opened on Colorado Day, August 1, 1984.

STAIRWAY TO THE STARS

Much of Georgetown's silver originated in the Argentine Mining District south of town. A long arduous trip by mule-drawn wagons carried ore down from the mines and supplies up to them. Thus, the stage was set for the birth of one of Colorado's most improbable railroads, the Argentine Central.

Methodist minister Edward Wilcox, who vowed that the railroad would never run on Sunday as long as he owned it, began construction of the Argentine Central in 1905. The railway's track connected with the Colorado & Southern at Silver Plume and was so steep that only novel-geared steam locomotives could negotiate it. The line reached the mining camp of Waldorf (elevation eleven thousand feet) in early 1906, only because of an exceptionally mild winter. Most years would see it closed for six months, covered in a cold, white blanket.

By then, tourism was recognized as an important source of revenue in the area; thus, the tracks were extended to the summit of Mt. McClellan in late 1906 simply for the purpose of carrying sightseers to those lofty heights. Seven layers of railroad track (including the Georgetown Loop) could be seen from one point on the railroad. Because of this staircase-like vision, the railroad was nicknamed "Stairway to the Stars." A dozen or more trains could reach the summit on a busy day with passengers arriving on special trains from Denver. What a thrill it must have been to arrive at Denver Union Station on a train from the sweltering flatlands and be frolicking in the snow on top of Mt. McClellan less than five hours later! Mining traffic was also substantial, as the railroad had been constructed to pass every mine in the Argentine Mining District.

Mining became a murmur and tourism dried up, however, at the end, the Argentine Central carried only tourists for less than two months out of the year.

With the United States' entry into World War I in 1918, the trains ceased their mountain-climbing antics. It must have been heartbreaking to see the trains to Mt. McClellan expire after only thirteen years. Even after the Argentine Central's demise, snow prevented access to the railroad, and the last rails were not removed until 1920.

The Argentine Central, pictured here in the early 1900s, was one of two Colorado railroads that ran to the very pinnacle of a mountain simply for the purpose of transporting sightseers. In the typical exuberance of the times, a hotel and other amenities were proposed at the summit of Mt. McClellan but were never constructed. (Courtesy, Denver Public Library, Western History Collection, MCC-681. Photo by L. C. McClure.)

The railroad caboose carried the conductor's office, where paperwork on freight shipments was completed. No longer needed for its intended purpose, this caboose on the Georgetown Loop Railroad simply reinforces the illusion of the railroad's historical setting.

tom would be preserved. The society and a private company began reconstruction of the railroad in 1973. A million-dollar grant saw the 1983 completion of a new Devil's Gate Bridge, with train service over the entire Georgetown Loop beginning in 1984. Reconstruction was slow and arduous but done with close attention to historic detail. The modern-day passenger is treated to the same sights as early-day miners. A stopover along the route allows for a tour deep into the gut of the Lebanon Mine. The mine's surface buildings have been re-created and the Lebanon Mill preserved.

Exploring: The Georgetown Loop Railroad

U.S. 6 follows the route of the Colorado Central west from Golden through Clear Creek canyon. A side trip north on Colorado Highway 119 follows the Central City branch. Legalized gambling has greatly changed the overall ambiance of Central City and Black Hawk. West of the junction with Highway 119 is Idaho Springs, where you can see a narrow-gauge steam locomotive display and other mining era remnants. Farther west is Georgetown and the far-famed Loop. Be sure to ride the Georgetown Loop Railroad and take the mine tour. A visitors center near the Georgetown end of the Loop helps guests interpret history. There are also many restored buildings in Georgetown worth exploring, including the old railroad depot. Most of the Loop is visible from a scenic overlook between Silver Plume and Georgetown, which is accessible from the eastbound lanes of Interstate 70. Look across the valley to see the location of the lowest switchbacks on the Argentine Central Railway, which provided much ore traffic to the Colorado Central.

CHAPTER 2

CLIMAX EXPRESS

The Denver, South Park & Pacific Railroad

Among all Colorado's narrow-gauge railroads, two stand out in the minds of enthusiasts. Both scratched their way through remote and spectacular mountains with the optimistic speculation of freight and passenger traffic. That optimism quickly vanished, however, and neither had much economic impact. With little revenue, both struggled with antique nineteenth-century equipment well into the twentieth century. One, the Rio Grande Southern Railroad, is examined in chapter 11. The other, the Denver, South Park & Pacific, was a 350-mile streak of rust that crested five mountain passes—three over eleven thousand feet high. Except in a few raucous mining years, it typically lost money. Yet, it survived until the late 1930s, with its rails firmly affixed to the capital city of Denver. The Denver, South Park & Pacific had several names over the years, but everyone just called it the "South Park," after the wide mountain valley southwest of Denver. Eventually the railroad became part of the Colorado & Southern.

A Rivalry Among Cities

The plethora of Colorado front-range railroads was as much a competition among cities as among trains. Loveland hoped the Colorado Central would retain the capital in Golden. Palmer had headquartered the Denver & Rio Grande in Colorado Springs. It fell to former governor of the Colorado territory, Dr. John Evans, to advance the cause of Denver with the South Park.

Initial construction of the South Park stalled at Morrison in 1874, just a few miles west of Denver. Construction would not resume until 1878 when the lure of Leadville's

Facing page: St. Elmo retains much of its nineteenth-century charm on the South Park's eastern approach to the Alpine Tunnel.

Inset: Looking east toward the western portal of the Alpine Tunnel, enginehouse ruins stand on the right while the coaling platform is on the left side of the photo. The enginehouse originally sheltered a turntable from brutal weather. When locos became longer, the short indoor turntable was abandoned and another longer turntable was built outdoors nearer to the tunnel portal.

riches inspired investors to dig deeper into their wallets. The trains crested Kenosha Pass and dropped into South Park, arriving at Como in 1879.

The first important destination was to have been the mines at Fairplay, but those mines were now old news compared to the Leadville bonanza. The narrow track continued over Trout Creek Pass to reach the Arkansas River. There the South Park's narrow-gauge trains would travel north to Leadville on the tracks of the Denver & Rio Grande. In return, the Rio Grande's narrow-gauge trains would be allowed to travel to Gunnison on the yet-to-be-constructed tracks of the South Park.

The South Park did not reach Gunnison until 1882 by a most impractical route through the Alpine Tunnel. By that time, ownership of both railroads had changed, and neither the Rio Grande nor the South Park trusted each other or their joint trackage agreement. The Rio Grande built a much easier-to-operate railroad over Marshall Pass into Gunnison. The South Park built its own sky-high line to Leadville. South Park rails went north from Como and crossed Boreas Pass to reach Breckenridge, where they circled around to enter Leadville from the north, climbing Fremont Pass near the town of Climax.

Lost in the Mountains

The South Park mainline was never completed, partly because it never really knew where it was going. As new "hot" mining camps replaced old, the tracks wandered around the mountains searching for a destination. The railroad was originally incorporated to reach the mining districts of the San Juan Mountains in southwestern Colorado on its way to the Pacific Ocean. Distracted by Leadville's prosperity, the South Park was too late to beat the Rio Grande to the San Juans. Instead, it headed for Gunnison where there was new promising economic news. Routes were again postulated to the Pacific. One proposed line would serve Lake City, Ouray, and Rico on its way through Arizona to the great western ocean. A second would travel north over Ohio Creek Pass, through Grand

After the Leadville boom erupted, the South Park was distracted from its original destination of Fairplay. Fairplay would eventually be served but only by a branch—one that never dropped below ten thousand feet! In this 1880s photograph, a train waits at London Junction on the Fairplay branch. (Courtesy, Denver Public Library, Western History Collection, WHJ-741. Photo by W. H. Jackson.)

Pachyderm Pusher

One of the most-repeated anecdotes about the South Park concerns circus elephants. A South Park locomotive stalled on a steep hill in a driving snowstorm while carrying a circus to a mountain town. Elephants pushed the train to the top of the hill, assisting the overloaded locomotive. There are at least four references to this incident, each claiming it happened in a different place. One story states the train failed on Kenosha Pass on its way to Gunnison in the early 1880s. Other stories locate the stalled train just west of the Alpine Tunnel on Boreas Pass and nearer Fremont Pass. Almost surely the incident did occur, and the story was so good that more than one storyteller adopted it.

This illustration of the elephant incident appeared in the June 1941 issue of Railroad Magazine.

Junction, across Utah, and on to salt water. It was the Rio Grande, however, that would build west out of Gunnison, reaching Lake City, Montrose, Grand Junction, and even Salt Lake City. Although the second-place South Park did actually start building over Ohio Creek Pass, only a few coal mines were served by this truncated line, and its narrow-gauge trains never traveled any closer to the West Coast than Baldwin, just north of Gunnison.

Hub of the South Park

After Denver, Como was the most important railroad center on the South Park. Three divisions of the railroad converged there. One division went east to Denver, another north to Leadville, and a third west to Gunnison. Nearby coal mines provided fuel for hungry locomotives as well as traffic to distant cities. On the edge of frigid and isolated South Park, at almost ten thousand feet, Como was not the ideal setting for the 350 railroad families living there. The railroad provided some amenities, including a library and a barbershop, but it was a hard place.

Day and night, the toy-like trains scurried about the Como yard, arriving from and departing to three points of the compass. Short freight trains of fewer than a dozen cars would require three or four locomotives and crews to push and pull them over the mountains. A nineteen-stall roundhouse and other facilities serviced the helper engines added at Como to nudge the little trains over steep mountain passes. The rotary snowplow stationed in Como required assistance as well: Up to five locomotives would prod the mechanical snow eater through the mountainous drifts when the track had to be cleared. Before federal law limited hours of service for railroad employees, trainmen would work almost around the clock, sleep but a few hours, and be called for service again.

The Alpine Tunnel and Boreas Pass were sometimes closed for years, as the economics of expensive maintenance and snow removal conflicted with the area's meager traffic. In 1910, Boreas Pass, Trout Creek Pass, and the Alpine Tunnel were all closed. Boreas Pass would open again in a few years, but the Gunnison extension was doomed. Como had seen the end of good times. Loyal employees who had braved the dangers of runaway trains in snowy blizzards were rewarded with layoffs or termination. Como's population dwindled to fewer than a dozen families by 1911.

Nothing Could Save It

When the Gunnison division closed in 1910, the South Park's last significant traffic source was Leadville. By then, Leadville was also served by two standard-gauge railroads. The wider tracks of the Colorado Midland had arrived in Leadville, and the Denver & Rio Grande widened its rails to remain competitive. Only the

Right: The remains of a water tank decorate the South Park grade on the western approach to the Alpine Tunnel. Steam locomotives have a mighty thirst, and water tanks—or their ruins—dot the Colorado mountains.

Below: Coal was stored on this platform and shoveled, by hand, into locomotive tenders.

These steel bands once held together a water tank perched on this wooden platform inside the Alpine Tunnel enginehouse. The tank was inside to keep the water from freezing solid.

South Park trundled along using the uncompetitive narrow-gauge technology that had been all the rage just forty years before.

Despite these problems, the South Park might have flourished had mining prospered. As elsewhere, reliance on precious-metal mining doomed the railroad. Carrying livestock, coal, feldspar, stone, and numerous other commodities, the South Park was more diverse than the Colorado Central. Regardless, nothing could compensate for the loss of the great mining camps. The last train from Denver to Leadville ran in 1937.

Action at Leadville

Molybdenum was discovered near the future Climax mine in 1895. "Moly" was a valuable mineral used in the manufacture of steel and had become an important traffic source by 1937. For this reason, the railroad from Leadville to Climax was not dismantled with the rest of the South Park. Besides shipping moly, the railroad transported the machinery and supplies Climax needed to expand production. After the mainline was closed in 1937, narrow-gauge trains served Climax from Leadville instead of from Denver. The Leadville connection with the standard-gauge Rio Grande required the needless expense of transferring freight between narrow-gauge and standard-gauge cars. The narrow gauge was irredeemable, and the fourteen miles between Climax and Leadville were widened in 1943.

Two steam locomotives operated this branch line train until 1962. By then, they were the last standard-gauge steam locomotives to operate on a major U.S. railroad. Diesels replaced steam, and the last vestige of the South Park continued operating until the Climax mine closed in 1987. In 1986, modern diesel locomotives had made their last run to Climax, dressed in the green and black of the Burlington Northern. With the economy of Leadville at a low ebb, the track to Climax was then sold to the Leadville, Colorado & Southern Railroad, which continues to operate passenger trains from Leadville to Climax today.

Exploring: The Leadville, Colorado & Southern Railroad

West of Denver on U.S. Highway 285, the U.S. Forest Service has a railroad display on Kenosha Pass. Continuing west on U.S. 285, you'll find Como, which still harbors the six stone stalls of the original South Park roundhouse. The Boreas Pass line is now an unpaved road north from there. Bakers Tank continues to stand along the old railroad on Boreas Pass, and an original rotary snowplow is displayed in Breckenridge where the Boreas Pass road again joins pavement.

At Leadville, don't miss the chance to ride a train over the South Park route on the Leadville, Colorado & Southern. On the trip to Climax, you'll pass French Gulch Tank, last used for filling a steam locomotive's tender in 1962. One of the last two steam locomotives to reach Climax is displayed at the Leadville depot. The Leadville, Colorado & Southern roundhouse is all that remains of the original structure.

The town of St. Elmo lies on the approach to the eastern portal of the Alpine Tunnel. The western portal can be reached from Parlin, east of Gunnison on U.S. Highway 50. A road leads from Parlin to Pitkin, where the pavement ends. Near Pitkin, the South Park grade is an unpaved road providing access to the west side of the Alpine Tunnel. A water tank still stands near Woodstock, and several structures are being restored by the Forest Service at the tunnel's western portal.

THE ALPINE TUNNEL

Just short of two thousand feet in length, the great Alpine Tunnel was a spectacular construction project completed in 1882 by the South Park at the inhospitable altitude of almost twelve thousand feet. Its route through decomposed granite, originally thought to be solid rock, required thousands of feet of redwood supports and lining—enough lumber to construct a small town. The western portal included a turntable, a large stone enginehouse with a water tank tucked inside out of the cold, a boarding house, a coaling platform, and other structures.

The tunnel's eastern approach was built on a slope facing north, where drifting snows blocked the tracks in winter and would not melt until late summer—if then. The western approach required that a rock shelf be blasted out of a precipitous cliff. Temperatures reached 40 degrees below zero, and engines slipped on the steep, icy grades. Dozens were killed both in the construction and operation of the bore; thirteen were killed by an avalanche at Woodstock on the west side, and four were killed by locomotive fumes while trying to reopen the tunnel in 1895.

So snowy was the eastern approach that in 1890 the Union Pacific staged a contest there between mechanized snowplows built by the Jull Manufacturing Company and the Leslie Brothers Manufacturing Company. The Leslie won with ease and became the standard railroad rotary snowplow used in the United States.

Above: The snow-crushed ruins of the Alpine Tunnel boarding house lie in the foreground at over eleven thousand feet above sea level.

Top: A one-car South Park train has just left the west portal of the Alpine Tunnel in this photograph from the end of the nineteenth century. (*Courtesy, Denver Public Library, Western History Collection, MCC-3233. Photo by L. C. McClure.*)

Above: *South Park trains delivered patrons to this hotel on the Platte River. Before air conditioning, well-to-do families would send mom and the kids to spend an extended holiday in the cool mountains where dad would join them on weekends.*

Left: *A restored Bakers Tank still stands on the Boreas Pass line of the South Park.*

Above: You can spot the South Park's shelf-like grade, called the Palisades, on the western approach to the Alpine Tunnel. It appears halfway up the mountainside on the right of this photo.

Facing page: Serving molybdenum mines, this portion of the South Park from Leadville to Climax continued operating as a standard-gauge railroad after narrow-gauge trains stopped running. Green Burlington Northern diesel locomotives also once departed from Leadville in the shadow of Colorado's highest mountains.

Above: Standing over the western portal of the Alpine Tunnel, you can see the railroad grade exit the remains of the wooden snowshed that once protected little trains as they emerged from the tunnel into howling gales.

Left: Leadville's economy turned sour when the Climax mine closed. As part of the mining camp's resurrection as a tourist destination, passengers again travel the route of the South Park on the Leadville, Colorado & Southern.

PART II

NOSEBLEED LINES

There you stand, facing the great wall of the Rocky Mountains' eastern edge. You've just been given the job of locating hundreds of miles of railroad through the range's heart. There are no topographic maps, no helicopters, and no global positioning system—only you and the mountains.

These were the challenges facing the early civil engineers who located Colorado's first railroads. They didn't always place a railroad in the perfect location, but it was often amazing they found any route at all. Inadequate capital required that railroads be placed so that they were least expensive to build, even if that meant expensive operations on long, steep grades and frequent closures by unimaginable snows. Moving the railroad to a better spot could wait until the profits rolled in. Some lines became profitable enough to be improved, but most high-altitude lines simply became backcountry roads or trails.

All of Colorado's mountain railroads were, and are, high. The following part illustrates the extreme altitude of Colorado's railroads and the trains that crawled over the slopes of America's most famous mountain, Pikes Peak. On its eastern slope, passengers still ride the highest railroad in the northern hemisphere, the Manitou & Pike's Peak Railway. The northern, western, and southern slopes of Pikes Peak are haunted by the ghosts of three railroad lines that once served the gold camps clustered around Cripple Creek. One of these, the Colorado Midland, continued westward to cross three mountain passes. Finally, this part concludes with another line, the Denver, Northwestern & Pacific, or "Moffat," a railroad north of the Midland that spent miles above the clouds before a six-mile-long tunnel was bored through the Continental Divide to avoid the white hell of winter.

Built in 1897, number 4 is the only operating steam locomotive left on the Manitou & Pike's Peak.

CHAPTER 3

TRAINS WITH TEETH
The Manitou & Pike's Peak Railway

Yes, this railroad really does have teeth—around half a million of them—that help its trains climb to the 14,110-foot summit of Pikes Peak from Manitou Springs. In some ways, the Manitou & Pike's Peak Railway

is the most under-appreciated of Colorado's historic railroads. It never served gold or silver mines but was built to carry people. Known affectionately to locals as the "Cog," it is a railroad of superlatives. It is the highest railway in North America, the highest cog railway in the world, and the second-highest railroad of any kind anywhere. Its trains have struggled upward since 1891 without a rest. Like a string of pearls, the Manitou & Pike's Peak Railway dangles from the neck of "America's Most Famous Mountain," reflecting the gems of human activity that show the optimism of nineteenth-century entrepreneurs.

Gravity Down, Steam Up

Major John Hulbert of Manitou Springs was the visionary who promoted the Cog to completion. According to legend, Zalmon Simmons was vacationing in Manitou Springs when Hulbert presented him with his pitch for building the Cog. Simmons was persuaded to ride a burro to the summit the next day. The discomfort of this ride convinced the mattress maker from Wisconsin to bankroll construction of this unique railroad.

Grading the roadbed started at the summit on September 25, 1889. After all, it's easier to push dirt downhill than up. Even so, work had to be suspended above timberline after the November snow deepened. Laborers, making just two dollars a day, lasted only three weeks before the grueling work without sufficient oxygen started to take its toll. All work had to be done with picks, shovels, and

Facing page: Climbing the steep grade below Windy Point clearly shows off the power of cog railroad technology.

Inset: Just above the depot, four track switches deliver trains to the shops and sheds. The complexity of cog trackwork precludes the technology's use, except in very special circumstances.

wheelbarrows. Even horses couldn't work on the steep, rugged grade. After the grade was complete, track was laid from the bottom up. Steam locomotives pushed up flatcar loads of steel components and wooden crossties to be assembled into cog track. The line was finished on October 20, 1890, after a surprisingly short thirteen months of brutal effort.

About Those Teeth …

Why was cog railroad technology chosen to climb Pikes Peak? An ordinary railroad was considered, but because it could not climb as steeply, an ordinary train would have had to navigate many loops of track, two switchbacks, and one spiral along its 27-mile length. The Cog ran only 8.9 miles in a more direct path to the summit, and promised to be less expensive to build and operate.

Early in the history of railroading, some engineers did not believe that steel wheels would adhere adequately to steel rails. Despite these misgivings, adhesion railroads are now virtually universal worldwide. Before success was assured, both English and American inventors built track with center rails—rack rails with teeth that the locomotive's gear or cog wheel could firmly grip. The expense of that extra-stout-toothed rail and the difficulty of switching tracks doomed cog railroads for all but the Swiss. The Swiss had little choice, for they had to make trains climb through their mountainous country or they would not have railroads at all. Most cog railroad technical developments are attributed to Swiss engineers, and many of the world's cog railways are located in Switzerland. Swiss engineer Roman Abt invented the cog system used on the Manitou & Pike's Peak.

Manitou Springs

An ornate depot still greets Cog passengers as it did over a century ago in Manitou Springs where the route of the classic railway begins. Waiting for their train, most visitors fail to notice that the railroad's small office actually straddles Ruxton Creek. Neither do they know that this was the trolley shelter. Once, you could hear the whir of electric motors as tiny streetcars came to rest on the other side of the creek. Visitors of the early twentieth century merely walked through the trolley shelter over that creek to board the railway.

Above: This wooden coach was restored for the nation's bicentennial, and the steam loco was rescued from retirement in a museum.

Facing page: Decorated with tools, this vital work train goes about its daily business, following in the footsteps of the construction crews that built the Manitou & Pike's Peak Railway.

Minnehaha

Imagine building a house on hundreds of acres in the wilds of a mountainside, with access only by burro trail up an impossibly steep creek. Then, imagine seeing an impossibly steep railroad built just twenty-five feet from your front door. Such was the image presented to pioneer photographer William E. Hook who built what he thought would be a secluded home at Artist's Glen, just downhill from Minnehaha. Hook was so upset with the invasion of the Cog line that he unsuccessfully tried to legally block its construction. His relationship with the railroad was unusual to say the least. Although it ended his wilderness solitude, it also provided customers to buy his photographs.

A waterfall still trickles at Minnehaha, the location of a siding, which allows trains traveling in opposite directions to pass each other. Here, rustic summer homes once provided a cool refuge for residents of the Great Plains states, the Pikes Peak Alpine Laboratory stood as a base for botanical researchers, and you could hear the hum of generators as the Pikes Peak Power Company provided "juice" to the developing communities below.

A steep hill just west of Minnehaha earned a colorful nickname. It was a hot day, and the fireman of the cog steam locomotive stopped for a cold beer on

America's Most Famous Mountain

Lieutenant Zebulon Montgomery Pike sighted Pikes Peak from what is now the city of Pueblo and greatly overestimated its height at over 18,000 feet. At 14,110 feet, Pikes Peak is only the thirty-second highest of Colorado's mountains, yet it is "America's Most Famous Mountain." As the easternmost peak in Colorado's front range, it was a beacon to pioneers—often the first mountain they saw. It became a symbol of Colorado and the golden riches secreted away in its mountains. Surely you remember that drawing of the covered wagon in your fourth-grade history book that said "Pikes Peak or Bust" on its side.

From the top of Pilot Knob, you can spot much of the Manitou & Pike's Peak Railway. Follow the track up from the train in this photograph, then to the left and up to spot the straight track through Mountain View. On the left-hand side of the photo, you can barely see the beginning of the grade of the Big Hill. The railroad disappears as it climbs the remaining distance to Pikes Peak, the highest point visible.

Hotel guests once bustled around a depot, post office, lunch counter, gift shop, and stables at Half-Way House. Today, a railroad siding keeps company with a lonely water tank there.

his way home. One thing led to another and he stayed just a little too late, making his wife none too pleased with his tardy arrival home. Passing through Minnehaha with a bad headache the next morning, the fireman soon hit the first long stretch of the steepest grade on the Cog line. Shoveling coal in earnest to keep the locomotive pushing the coach full of passengers, is it any wonder he and his fellow trainmen named this hill "Son of a Gun"? (The firemen actually called it something slightly saucier.)

Half-Way House

Passenger trains were running to Half-Way House on the partially completed railroad by the middle of the summer of 1890. Today, a restored siding, a sign, an old steam loco water tank, and an empty meadow mark the location of the depot that once anchored this spot. The very rustic hotel, without indoor plumbing, provided shelter for ten dollars a week. Visitors refreshed themselves at the depot lunch counter, bought souvenirs at the curio shop, or mailed letters from the U.S. Post Office that serviced "Half Way, Colorado"—although this place is actually not halfway between anything! The owner of

the Half-Way House Hotel, Thomas Palsgrove, just liked the name.

Almost immediately uphill is Ruxton Park. Palsgrove platted a subdivision here and posted a sign that enticed railroad passengers to buy a lot of their own. Ruins of log cabins for summer visitors can be seen today, as can a couple of homes built for caretakers of the Colorado Springs watershed and a small hydroelectric plant. A stone building still protects the plant, which is the oldest operating hydro plant west of the Mississippi River.

Mountain View

Mountain View deserves its name. Here, Cog passengers have their first view of the Pikes Peak summit, until now obscured by canyon walls and lower mountain peaks. There are actually two locations with the name Mountain View. The other, lower Old Mountain View, was home to the *Pikes Peak Daily News*. Starting in 1891, the newspaper was published in Old Mountain View whenever the trains ran. Seven of its eight pages were pre-printed with local advertising and the history of the region. A newspaper employee would board the train at Manitou Springs and collect

PLOWING SNOW

Snow removal is an art on the Manitou & Pike's Peak. Fifteen-foot drifts are not uncommon, and millions of cubic feet of snow have to be moved each spring. In years past, two months of snow removal often ended in a late spring storm that closed the line for another month. A flat car equipped with an inclined metal "plow point" would be pushed under the snow and backed out with about ten tons to be unloaded by hand shovelers. Difficult work at any altitude, workers willing to suffer at twelve thousand feet were increasingly scarce by the 1960s. By the end of that decade, the railroad added a hydraulic mechanism to the flat car to dump the snow to one side.

The Cog built an unsuccessful rotary snowplow in the 1950s with technology copied from mainline railroads. In the 1970s, the railroad added a new rotary snowplow, which was a huge version of a home snow blower. Although the plow was a great improvement, compacted snow still became as hard as concrete after a long winter. The rotary plow merely polished that snow to a high gloss unless it was first loosened with explosives. Most recently, the Cog has periodically plowed through the entire winter, preventing the white powder from hardening, but by no means is the white beast of winter tamed. The new rotary plow stands guard every spring at its own siding at Windy Point, protecting passengers from being marooned on the summit by a sudden storm.

Above: Tons of snow fly hundreds of feet through the air as it is cleared by a rotary snowplow.

Top: The new rotary snowplow of the Manitou & Pike's Peak nears the summit after grinding through drifts lower down.

the names of all the passengers. That information was then dropped at the newspaper's alpine office, and the names were quickly set in type and printed on the newspaper's one blank page. By the time the train returned downhill, the "personalized" newspapers were ready for sale to the train's passengers for the extravagant sum of twenty-five cents.

America the Beautiful

The Cog's track glides around a beautifully shaped curve, Grecian Bend, named for the bustles worn by Victorian-era women. The longest stretch of the steepest part of the track lies ahead with the uninspired name of the Big Hill. Halfway up this hill, the forest suddenly falls away as the trains cross timberline. The view of mountains and plains to the east inspired Katherine Lee Bates to write the poem that later became the song "America the Beautiful."

The tracks crawl around to the south side of the mountain and pass a small stone building. This was the Windy Point section house, one of several on the line. Years ago, when many more men were required to maintain the track, the route was divided into sections, each maintained by a section crew. To save the long, arduous, and expensive steam-driven trip to work, crews would live in section houses near the track they maintained. At least one baby was born here, at twelve thousand feet above sea level, to a foreman's wife. Section crews still maintain the track but diesel-powered work trains deliver them to their employment each morning.

Here grow fields of tiny alpine flowers. Years ago, a girl would board the train at Windy Point and sell small bouquets of wildflowers to passengers. "Windy" was also the location of the highest water tank on the line, where steam locomotives filled up for their final push to the summit. You can still see the little reservoir and pump house ruins where an employee spent the summer stoking the steam boiler to pump water uphill. Water tanks lower on the mountain were fed with the help of gravity, the preferred technology of the time.

Waiting to depart the summit, a glossy red Cog train reflects spring's snow.

The Tortoise and the Hare

The Cog holds the record for both the fastest and the slowest employees. Early on, railroad workers discovered they could scoot downhill on their shovels balanced on the center rack rail. This primitive technology developed to provide a smoother ride on a small seat, or "toboggan," on one outside rail, balanced with an outrigger on the rack rail. When descending from the top, the daredevils had to portage around four track switches that could not be negotiated by these contraptions. Allegedly, the record top speed was fifty miles an hour. Imagine flying along just inches above the rail at this speed with no helmet or other protective gear. At least one fatality occurred, and the practice has been banned for a very long time.

The slower counterpart of these adventuresome workers had a much more mundane job. For decades, an employee had the tedious task of carrying a bucket of lubricant up the track to manually dab some on each tooth of the rack rail, because, like all gears, the center rack rail had to be lubricated. The lubricant was called "dope" and the man was called the "Doper." Starting at Manitou and walking uphill, all went well for the Doper for a few hundred yards until the dope cooled and congealed. He would build a fire to heat the dope and then repeat the process, a few hundred yards at a time. He straggled onto the summit in about a month only to start all over again. Today's trains have automatic lubricators that slicken the rack rail as they run their normal schedule.

Above, right: Each of the half million "teeth" on the Cog track were once individually lubricated.

Below: The very first toboggans used on the Cog line perched on the center rail and were balanced with poles. Here, an adventurous family slides down the track shortly after the railroad was built. (Courtesy, Ed and Nancy Bathke.)

Centenarian locomotive 4 steams quietly at the Manitou Springs depot.

The Summit

As the train pulls onto the summit, sharp-eyed travelers will notice the ruins of an old stone wall. Before anyone even dreamed of a train to the top of Pikes Peak, the U.S. Army Signal Service constructed a stone building here to monitor the weather. A trail and telegraph line connected this remote outpost to civilization below. No longer in use when the railroad finally crested the mountain, the old stone building became the railroad's depot. It was expanded over the years, and travelers could actually spend the night there. A steel observation tower, again for twenty-five cents, provided a better view west over the flat area of the summit. Today the tower is gone, along with the old summit house, but the views still entice. To the north, the aptly named Bottomless Pit opens onto a view of Rampart Reservoir and the city of Woodland Park. Colorado Springs and Kansas lie to the east. Observant visitors can also spot some of the mines on Gold Hill to the southwest near Cripple Creek.

Exploring: Rails Above the Clouds

Old cog steam locos are on display in Manitou Springs' Memorial Park, east of downtown on Manitou Avenue, and near the Cog's depot. Drive south on Ruxton Avenue to reach the depot. Part way up Ruxton, you'll see Ruxton Creek on your left. The dirt path across the creek is the route of the old trolley car to the depot. At one point, you'll cross the location of the Colorado Midland's trestle. The trestle was removed in the 1960s, but you can still see some of the stonework used to support it. Of course, you should also be sure to ride the Cog to the summit of Pikes Peak.

CIVILIZATION, TWO MILES UP
The Trains of Cripple Creek

The Cripple Creek & Victor Mining District is an excellent example of Colorado's many stratospheric railroad locations. Not a lonely mountain pass in the middle of the wilderness, the District was a mini-metropolis of cities, suburbs, mines, and mills. Trains swarmed like ants at a picnic over miles of track on Gold Hill, an area roughly east of the line between Cripple Creek and Victor, where all the gold in the region was found. With a peak population of fifty-five thousand, crowds packed the streets of the District—men on the way to work, women to shop, and children to school. There were three dozen churches (but twelve dozen saloons!), nineteen schools, hundreds of businesses, and sixteen newspapers to satisfy the hunger for information in this two-mile-high outpost of civilization.

Cripple Creek

Bob Womack struck gold in 1890 in Poverty Gulch near the present site of Cripple Creek. In a mere ten years, Cripple Creek grew to be the fourth-largest city in Colorado, while its southern neighbor, Victor, was fifth largest. Cripple Creek was the center of business and wealth in the District. Industry and commerce hummed day and night, all two miles high. By 1900, eight thousand miners were hard at work there.

Well-heeled mine owners could phone the opera house for reservations or slip into a house of ill-repute on Myers Avenue. "Parlor houses" served wealthier men, while ordinary miners frequented cheaper brothels called "cribs." Writer Julian Street visited the town long after Cripple Creek's zenith, and his *Collier's Weekly* magazine article would dwell on the sordid past of Myers Avenue instead of the District's past glories. The outraged

Facing page: A Cripple Creek & Victor train skirts the western edge of Gold Hill.

Inset: Trolley cars once delivered miners to this high-altitude saloon at Midway on Gold Hill.

This Midland Terminal passenger train is on its way to the Cripple Creek depot in this photograph from 1896. Bob Womack discovered gold here at Poverty Gulch, triggering the gold rush that created this two-mile-high metropolis. (Courtesy, Denver Public Library, Western History Collection, P-1710. Photo by H. S. Poley.)

citizens of Cripple Creek temporarily renamed Myers Avenue. They called it "Julian Street."

The Burbs

Many towns, which we might call "suburbs" today, dotted Gold Hill. Victor, the City of Mines, was the second-largest city in the District. Not much smaller than Cripple Creek, it boasted schools, churches, two daily papers, and too many saloons. Most of the gold came from Victor, not from Cripple Creek. Gold was discovered there while excavating for the foundation of a building, and the owner made millions. Not all the mines were within the city, but many were within sight of Victor, just east on Battle Mountain. Victor was a working man's town, and miners toiled for the astonishing wage of three dollars per ten-hour day.

Goldfield, a working-class town like Victor, was the third largest in the District. Managing to stay free of the worst vices, it was a popular home for miners with families. On their one day off, miners would board the train for Pinnacle Park, located on the east side of Gold Hill at Cameron. Families would picnic, enjoy a few carnival rides, or see the bears in the zoo. More adult entertainment could be enjoyed at Gillett, north of the hill of gold, where a horse-racing track and casino provided the excitement. Gillett was home to twelve thousand souls as well as the shops of the Midland Terminal Railroad. It is best known as the site of the only authentic bullfight ever held in the United States.

Altman was the highest town in the District and the highest incorporated town in the United States at the nosebleed altitude of 10,620 feet. Even there in the clouds, a couple thousand residents once called Altman home. Other towns on Gold Hill included Stratton, Anaconda, Independence, Elkton, and Midway. Driving through the District today, it is hard to believe what was once here.

Early roads in the area, steep and muddy, were used by horse-drawn wagons. "Interurban" trains—

Left: This building in Cripple Creek is one of many that survived the ravages of time here and in nearby Victor.

Below: The District Museum, in the substantial Midland Terminal depot, preserves a treasure of railroad and mining history.

Above: Orange-tinged aspen surround a mine headframe as the little Cripple Creek & Victor train chugs past. Five hundred million dollars of gold, typically valued at twenty dollars per ounce, was extracted from Gold Hill.

Facing page: The First Baptist Church of Victor stands ready to save souls in a city that once had many more saloons than churches. Facing a difficult existence, miners found solace in the Lord or in alcohol.

electric trolley cars—circled the District and provided everyday transportation for the masses there, as they did in most of the United States. The District had two interurban lines. The low line connected Cripple Creek to Victor via Anaconda and Elkton. The high line perched on top of Gold Hill between Cripple Creek and Victor, but its trolleys rolled through Goldfield, Independence, and Midway. Commuting was as simple as stepping on a trolley car high in the Colorado Rockies.

Trains to Everywhere

Maps don't do justice to the intricacies of the railroads on Gold Hill. With three railroad companies and two trolley lines, tracks were a tangled maze, reminiscent of a major railroad center like Chicago and not a remote mountain niche. As many as fifty-eight passenger trains polished the rails between Cripple Creek and Victor each day. Supposedly, one could buy a ticket to Paris at the Cripple Creek depot—including the steamship coupons!

Railroads were the life-blood of the District. The Florence & Cripple Creek Railroad arrived in 1894, threading its way up Phantom Canyon, forty miles from Florence to Victor. Also called the "Gold Belt Line," it featured through Pullman cars to Denver on its narrow-gauge rails. The District's other two railroads were to be standard gauge.

The Colorado Midland was already serving the hamlet of Divide with a railroad line from Colorado

A passenger train exits one of many tunnels on the Short Line above a lower level of track, which can be seen on the left-hand side of this photograph from the early 1900s. After riding the Short Line in 1901, President Theodore Roosevelt was quoted as saying it was "the ride that bankrupted the English language." This widely publicized quote swamped the railroad with tourists wanting to experience its scenic wonders. (Courtesy, Denver Public Library, Western History Collection, MCC-89. Photo by L. C. McClure.)

Springs to points west. The Midland Terminal built south from Divide, swung around Gold Hill to Victor, and chugged into Cripple Creek in 1895.

The last railroad to arrive was officially named the Colorado Springs & Cripple Creek District Railway, but everyone just called it the "Short Line." It struck out due west from Colorado Springs to Victor around the south face of Pikes Peak. From Victor, it turned north to follow the other two railroads into Cripple Creek, arriving in 1901.

Transition

Eventually, all District railroads came under common ownership. Washed out by a flood in 1912, the Gold Belt Line was never rebuilt. Its owners chose wisely. Narrow-gauge railroads were becoming uneconomical, and the District's fortunes were waning. The Short Line ran through remote and rugged country with no significant source of additional traffic. It was dismantled in 1920.

The Midland Terminal survived longest. After the Colorado Midland closed in 1917, the Midland Terminal's trains traveled through Divide all the way down to Colorado Springs. Now, it served the communities of Ute Pass as well as the District. Passengers rode the rickety rails until the 1930s. When the Carlton Mill was built near Victor in 1949, the railroad was no longer needed to carry ore to the mill near Colorado Springs, and the last Midland Terminal train slowly crept to its own funeral.

Exploring: The Cripple Creek & Victor Narrow Gauge Railroad

Paved Colorado Highway 67 follows the Midland Ter-

THE VERY NARROW GAUGE

In 1967, the Cripple Creek and Victor began its narrow construction on the Midland Terminal grade in Cripple Creek. Trains reached Anaconda in 1970, disturbing the ghosts that once worked in the mines and mills on the mountainsides, and continue to depart from the historic Bull Hill Depot, relocated next to the District Museum. The little trains run on cost-effective two-foot-gauge track, which has a connection to railroad history around Central City to the north. A two-foot-gauge railroad, the Gilpin Tram, connected Central City, Black Hawk, and nearby mining camps to the three-foot-gauge Colorado Central. In fact, Black Hawk had the only dual-gauge railroad yard in the country where *both* gauges were narrow. Three-foot-wide and two-foot-wide trains would share the same tracks by using a third rail inside the two outside rails.

Cripple Creek lies just beyond the Cripple Creek & Victor train. More substantial brick construction replaced wood in the commercial district after a major fire destroyed the town in 1896.

Right: Gold Hill is dotted with mining's remnants and honeycombed with miles of tunnels, some thousands of feet below ground. With the District producing ore so rich it had to be locked inside boxcars for shipment, both Cripple Creek and Victor had gold-mining stock exchanges.

Below: The Cripple Creek & Victor pulls into the town of Anaconda, now mostly a memory but once a city of churches, schools, stores, and mines, and home to one thousand souls. Anaconda burned in 1904 and was never rebuilt.

A Florence and Cripple Creek passenger train heads down Phantom Canyon where narrow-gauge Pullman cars rocked passengers to sleep on their way to Denver, in this photograph circa the turn of the twentieth century. (Courtesy, Denver Public Library, Western History Collection, MCC-421. Photo by L. C. McClure.)

minal south from Divide and is built on the old railroad grade in some places. You'll see a railroad tunnel, now bypassed by the highway, and roll through the Gillett town site, although there is little left.

Both Cripple Creek and Victor were rebuilt with brick after devastating fires in the last decade of the nineteenth century; thus, much is left in both cities. Although its atmosphere changed after gambling was again legalized, Cripple Creek still offers a wealth of historic buildings and other attractions. Ride the Cripple Creek & Victor Narrow Gauge Railroad from Cripple Creek to Anaconda. Tour the authentic Mollie Kathleen Mine and learn about the area at the nearby Pikes Peak Heritage Center. Explore the very informative District Museum, situated in the substantial multistory depot that once saw passengers depart on the Midland Terminal for the rest of the country.

Highway 67 between Cripple Creek and Victor is built on the Florence & Cripple Creek railroad grade and skirts the western edge of Gold Hill. Don't miss Victor. Although its trolleys vanished in the 1920s, there are many historic buildings in town, and legendary mines still stand on Battle Mountain. You can completely circle Gold Hill on a paved road passing the outskirts of Goldfield on your way back to Gillett.

The other railroad grades to the District are now unpaved roads. South of Victor, the Florence & Cripple Creek grade is the Phantom Canyon Road. Autos pass over an old railroad bridge and through an original tunnel. The grade of the Colorado Springs & Cripple Creek District is the Gold Camp Road. It is still the ride that "bankrupted the English language," as President Theodore Roosevelt once quipped.

CHAPTER 5

THROUGH THE MOUNTAINS, NOT AROUND

The Colorado Midland Railway

With trains climbing up both the South Platte and Arkansas Rivers, wagon commerce to Leadville and other mining camps quickly faded on Ute Pass, a route west from Colorado Springs. In the latter part of the nineteenth century, the inevitable question was asked: Why not build a railroad up Ute Pass? Initially conceived by Homer Fisher to serve his lumber business near Woodland Park—just eighteen miles west of Colorado Springs—the project expanded, true to the optimism of the time. Banker Irving Howbert attracted the attention of industrialist James J. Hagerman to bankroll the project. Without a single foot of railroad track yet laid, the planned route of the Colorado Midland was extended from Woodland Park to the mining camps of Leadville and Aspen, the Glenwood Springs coal fields, Salt Lake City, and, as usual, the Pacific Ocean.

As it would turn out, Hagerman's most important change in plans was to lay standard-gauge track instead of narrow-gauge. This decision would affect all Colorado railroads to come. When the Colorado Midland was finally built, its standard-gauge trains could directly connect the mountain mining camps to the rest of the United States on the same width track. Freight did not have to be moved between narrow-gauge and standard-gauge cars in a costly, time-consuming process. Passengers could stay soundly asleep in their Pullman berths no matter the train's destination. Building the Colorado Midland with the wider gauge forced the Rio Grande to widen its narrow tracks wherever it competed.

Facing page: Remnants of Douglass City, on the east side of the Colorado Midland's High Line, echo with the sounds of the eight rowdy saloons that once entertained the workers who built the Hagerman Tunnel. Today, the wagon road to Douglass City is part of a hiking trail.

Inset: At Douglass City you can find the remains of the powerhouse that provided compressed air for the drills used in the construction of the Hagerman Tunnel.

The Midland was built to connect Colorado Springs with western commerce. This goal was to be accomplished regardless of the lay of the land. The Midland crossed three mountain passes, one at 11,528 feet above sea level, and much of its route ran at dizzying elevations. Westbound trains rose above 8,000 feet before arriving at Woodland Park and didn't descend through that elevation again until almost reaching Basalt.

Built Backwards

One might have expected a railroad headquartered in Colorado Springs to be built from that city west. Instead, the section of track connecting Leadville and Aspen to Glenwood Springs was to be pushed over the mountains first. The owners of the Colorado Midland also owned coal lands near Glenwood Springs. Coal could be hauled from there to the mining camps of Leadville and Aspen, providing immediate revenue with which to build the rest of the railroad. In order to build the western section first, the Midland's competitors would have to carry supplies to this isolated area of railroad construction, and they were in no mood to do so at a reasonable price.

The original plan to build the western section first was eventually abandoned. More capital was raised, and construction started from Colorado Springs in 1886. The Midland reached Leadville at the end of August 1887. Unfortunately, both the Rio Grande and the South Park had already arrived in the boom camp. The Midland was the second to arrive in Glenwood Springs in late 1887 and second to Aspen in 1888, beaten to both towns by the Rio Grande.

On lower Ute Pass, trains threaded expensively constructed tunnel after tunnel on costly-to-operate steep grades. Striking out through Eleven-Mile Canyon, the locomotives reached and crossed South Park. The railroad crested Trout Creek Pass alongside the South Park, dropped down to the Arkansas River, and paralleled the Rio Grande into Leadville. West from Leadville, spectacular Hagerman Pass drained both the railroad's construction bankroll and snow-plowing skills. At Basalt, a branch of the line headed for Aspen, while the mainline trundled northwest to New Castle, just beyond Glenwood Springs. The Midland entered

When a Colorado Midland train descended Trout Creek Pass, its engineer and fireman had views of the Collegiate Range towering over Buena Vista.

Grand Junction on tracks jointly owned with the Rio Grande. Grand Junction was as close to the Pacific as the Midland would ever come.

Bad Investments

It cost $20 million to build the first standard-gauge railroad to challenge the Colorado mountains. The Midland's revenues for 1890 were an impressive $1.7 million, but unfortunately, after expenses, a mere $2,500 remained to be sent to the stockholders! These numbers were typical of many ill-conceived railroad ventures of the time, especially in Colorado where construction and operating costs were as high as the mountains the railroads climbed. In light of these hopeless numbers, Hagerman sold the Midland to the Santa Fe. With its tracks extending east from

UTE PASS

Along with Fountain Creek, a waterfall of resorts spilled down the eastern approach of Ute Pass. Visitors walked through the cool summer woodlands and danced the evening away to the sounds of the very best bands. Manitou Springs was a vacation destination from the very first runs of the Colorado Midland. The town of Cascade was the next resort community west of Manitou Springs. The elegant Ramona Hotel rose there in 1884, named after a novel by Helen Hunt Jackson. The carriage road to the summit of Pikes Peak started its climb from Cascade, as does today's Pikes Peak Highway.

Farther west, Green Mountain Falls also hosted summer guests. Escaping the heat of the plains, many people owned summer homes there, including circus entrepreneur P. T. Barnum. The westernmost resort town was Woodland Park, where visitors once arrived at the Colorado Midland depot to spend a few nights at one of the town's ornate hotels. Originally a logging town, Woodland Park has a spectacular view of the summit of Pikes Peak.

A Colorado Midland passenger train passes through Green Mountain Falls, with one of the large Ute Pass resort hotels visible at the left of this late-nineteenth-century photo above the depot. The gazebo encircled by a lake is still a landmark, although trains no longer thunder along its north shore. (Courtesy, Colorado Historical Society, CHS-J482. Photo by W. H. Jackson.)

Above: The High Line's tracks diverged here. The left-hand route was a spur that had originally been the proposed alignment for the Midland's mainline, but which would have required another tunnel. The mainline was actually built along the right-hand route, as it would be quicker and less expensive to construct.

Right: Ovens once manufactured charcoal to be carried to market by the Colorado Midland. These ovens are located on the west side of Hagerman Pass near Sellar, where the railroad had substantial facilities including a depot, water tank, coal chute, sand house, and stock pens.

Colorado Springs, the Santa Fe hoped the Midland would funnel traffic from the west to its parent railroad. The new owners made improvements to the line, including a longer but lower tunnel through the Continental Divide west of Leadville.

A Bright Spot

Encouraged by the Colorado Midland, the Midland Terminal built south from the town of Divide and reached the Cripple Creek area in 1894. So important was this connection that the Colorado Midland delivered track materials to the Midland Terminal and never asked for payment! The Colorado Midland and the nation were prosperous as the nineteenth century turned into the twentieth, but in 1901 a new railroad, the Short Line, began stealing some of the Colorado Midland's Cripple Creek traffic. When the Midland Terminal merged with the other Cripple Creek railroads, all traffic was diverted over the Short Line and virtually nothing reached the Colorado Midland at Divide.

The Colorado Midland lost its battle with the Rio Grande. It simply could not compete. The Rio Grande's easier route and lower operating costs gave it an insurmountable advantage. The Midland was saddled with small antique locomotives and rickety, old track. It just didn't have the money that the Rio Grande had. The Rio Grande eventually siphoned off all the through traffic between Glenwood Springs and the eastern plains. With through traffic gone, the mining camps waning, and automobiles becoming more common, the Midland was in trouble.

The War to End All Wars

World War I injected a small spurt of traffic into the Colorado Midland line but not enough to keep it alive. A. E. Carlton purchased the Midland at a foreclosure sale in April 1917. Carlton also controlled the

FLOWER PICKERS

In July 1887, five hundred excited members of the First Methodist Church of Colorado Springs clambered onto a chartered train for an excursion to Eleven-Mile Canyon. Thus began the tradition of wildflower excursions on the Midland that would create the most endearing memories of the railroad for many. Routes varied but often ended in a picnic in Eleven-Mile Canyon. On the return journey, the happy excursionists would pick wildflowers near the town of Divide at the summit of Ute Pass.

On June 15, 1901, the National Association of Local Freight Agents enjoyed a wildflower excursion. The huge Colorado Midland train ran in two sections, each with two locomotives. (Courtesy, Colorado Historical Society, CHS-B271. Photo by H. H. Buckwalter.)

THE HIGH LINE

Imagine traveling west from Leadville on a Colorado Midland train. Sipping your hot coffee, you catch glimpses of Turquoise Lake through the twelve-foot snowdrifts. Your train has been climbing since leaving Leadville, but now its labors start in earnest. It snakes back and forth across the mountainside in lariat-like loops to gain elevation. There seems to be nothing below your train as it crawls out onto the timbers of thousand-foot Hagerman Trestle, the longest in Colorado. Finally, you reach the safety of the Hagerman Tunnel, 11,500 feet above sea level. Bursting out into the sunlight again, your train gingerly picks its way down the descending track to Basalt.

By 1894, trains no longer struggled up to the Hagerman Tunnel. The almost two-mile-long Busk-Ivanhoe Tunnel had bypassed the High Line—the loops of track, creaking wooden trestles, and the Hagerman Tunnel itself. It was not at all unusual for railroad construction to be financed through several companies, and so it was with the lower Busk-Ivanhoe Tunnel. By 1899, the Colorado Midland was using the upper tunnel again, as it couldn't agree with the Busk-Ivanhoe owners on rates for the use of the lower bore. Unfortunately for the Midland, it began to snow in Leadville on January 24 of that year, and it seemed like it would never stop.

The Colorado Midland, mighty standard-gauge monarch of the mountains, was closed for seventy-eight days. All of Colorado's railroads struggled, but the Midland's crossing of the Continental Divide through the Hagerman Tunnel was especially bad. Men and plows strained for days, only to have their mark erased by yet more snow. These were truly steel men—cold, hungry, tired, and at war with snow itself. The trains must get through, they believed, because railroads were the source of public welfare. Towns ran short of coal and food. Citizens shivered, and their stomachs growled.

Much dangerous, expensive, and time-consuming snow removal would have been avoided had the Midland been able to use the Busk-Ivanhoe Tunnel. By May 1899, an agreement was reached for the use of the lower tunnel. Now superfluous, the spectacular railroad through the Hagerman Tunnel was soon dismantled.

This monster steam-powered rotary chews through a white blockade on the High Line's Hagerman Pass in this photograph from the turn of the twentieth century. On one occasion, men on skis dragged a five-hundred-pound casting from Leadville to the High Line to repair the snow-eating beast. (Courtesy, Colorado Historical Society, CHS-B264. Photo by H. H. Buckwalter.)

The docile demeanor of the High Line in summer belies the raging fury that descends on this land in winter.

consolidated railroads in Cripple Creek. As he had previously diverted traffic to the Short Line, he now diverted traffic back to his new railroad. Carlton had money, and his two-million-dollar restoration program promised a bright future for the Midland—at least until the United States government took control of the nation's railroads in early 1918 to aid the war effort. As often happened with Colorado's railroads, absentee control meant disaster. Bureaucrats in Washington saw the Midland as the shortest route across the mountains with no regard for its difficult crossing of three mountain passes. They diverted all traffic from the Rio Grande to the Midland in the name of efficiency. The Midland's steep grades, antique locomotives, and worn-out track proved unequal to the task, and the line soon became plugged with railroad cars. The U.S. government's response was to move all traffic back to the Rio Grande. The Midland was dead.

Its operations ceased in 1918, and in 1921, its spectacular track west from Divide was removed despite Carlton's fruitless efforts to sell the railroad.

Exploring: Wide Tracks and Wildflowers

The majestic stone roundhouse of the Colorado Midland stands where once it sheltered steam locomotives at the corner of U.S. Highway 24 and 21st Street in Colorado Springs. Visit the Ghost Town Museum across the parking lot from the roundhouse in an original Midland shop building. Driving west of Manitou Springs on U.S. 24, you can see several tunnels above and just south of the highway. Modified from its original appearance, the Divide station still stands. An unpaved road south of Lake George becomes the railroad grade, travels through original tunnels, and offers access to picnic areas in Eleven-Mile Canyon in the same locations where railroad wildflower excursions once ran.

At the summit of Trout Creek Pass, just southwest of Antero Junction on U.S. 24/285, you can plainly see a notch in a large earthen fill where the Midland's tracks crossed over the South Park's. Farther west, the Midland's grade is a scenic unpaved road overlooking Buena Vista. Another portion of the grade is an unpaved road offering access to several tunnels north of Buena Vista.

On the east side of Hagerman Pass, a road leads from Leadville to Turquoise Lake, where you can drive the unpaved railroad grade to the east portal of the Busk-Ivanhoe Tunnel, now called the Carlton Tunnel. Farther along, a hiking trail leads to the east portal of the Hagerman Tunnel. On the west side of Hagerman Pass, the Basalt station building still stands and an unpaved road leads to the western side of the tunnels.

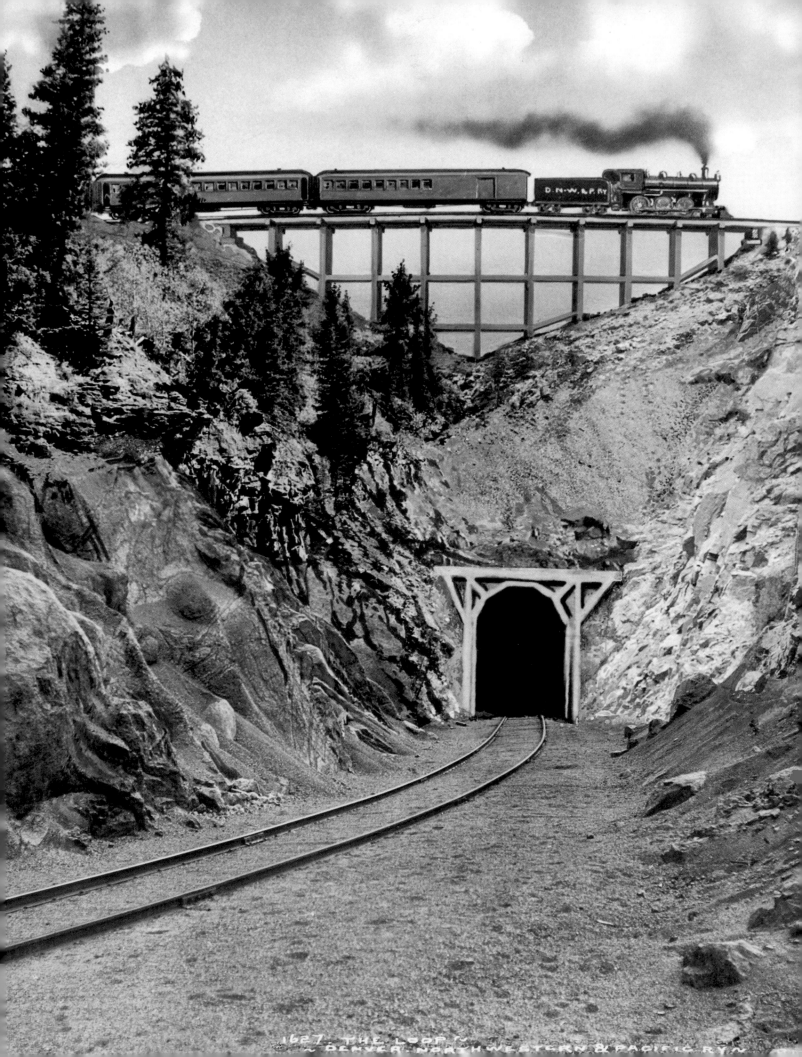

1627. THE LOOP.
DENVER, NORTHWESTERN & PACIFIC RY.

CHAPTER 6

CLIMBING ABOVE THE CLOUDS
The Denver, Northwestern & Pacific Railway

The Denver, Northwestern & Pacific's standard-gauge track over 11,660-foot Rollins Pass should have won the award for the most unlikely, most spectacular, and most costly-to-operate railroad in Colorado. The Argentine Central and Manitou & Pike's Peak reached greater heights, but the Denver, Northwestern & Pacific was a major carrier of freight and passengers, not a sightseeing line.

The Transcontinental Phantom

Even after the dawn of the twentieth century, the dream of a railroad from Denver to the Pacific was still alive in the guise of David Moffat. Moffat was Colorado's wealthiest citizen. After four decades, he had amassed a fortune through businesses ranging from mines to railroads and from trolleys to real estate. A remarkable man, Moffat's goal was as much to give Denver a locally controlled railroad as a path for western commerce. Moffat's men started surveying west from Denver in 1902. Although the route to northwestern Colorado would have several official names, starting as the Denver, Northwestern & Pacific, the locals always called it the "Moffat." The Rio Grande saw the Moffat as a competitor with a shorter route to the West and did all it could to physically, legally, and financially obstruct the new railroad. The Burlington, on the other hand, saw David

Facing page: Minutes earlier, the Denver, Northwestern & Pacific train on this trestle exploded out of the Loop Tunnel below it. Pictured here in an altered photograph from the early twentieth century, it has circled around and crosses over its own route. (Courtesy, Denver Public Library, Western History Collection, MCC-1627. Photo by L. C. McClure.)

Inset: Eastbound Moffat trains entered the Loop Tunnel on the grade pictured in the lower right of this photograph. After passing through the bore, trains continued uphill on a spiral of track and would cross the trestle shown at the left. Had he stood here seventy years earlier, the creator of this image would have seen the locomotive in the photo on the facing page heading toward him.

Moffat's railroad as its western outlet from Denver to the Pacific and encouraged its construction.

Tunnels, Tunnels Everywhere

Two and a half dozen tunnels were holed through the ribs of South Boulder Canyon before the Moffat's tracks reached Tolland in the spring of 1903. Some proved so unstable, they were abandoned before completion. Many required heavy timbering to keep the moving earth in check. These wooden supports would become a maintenance nightmare as well as provide fuel for tunnel fires, some of which proved deadly to the men of the Moffat.

With Moffat personally footing the bill and money in short supply, the next tunnel needed—a 2.6-mile titan—was out of the question. Instead, a temporary track crept up a sinuous path over Rollins Pass, because the railroad had to reach the coal mines of northwestern Colorado soon. In theory, income from moving those black diamonds would pay for the main tunnel later. The temporary line over Rollins Pass was finished by 1904.

Trains reached Hot Sulphur Springs in 1905, and the locomotive whistle sounded in Kremmling by 1906. Arrival in a new town always meant a celebration with bands, games, food, and speeches. This area, known as Middle Park, had no competing railroad, so the Moffat was critically important to its economy and quality of life. Trips to Denver had once been several-day ordeals by horse and wagon over precipitous mountain roads; or, in the winter, a lung-pounding snowshoe over Berthoud Pass to the narrow-gauge Colorado Central line. By comparison, the Moffat offered a comfortable trip measured in hours.

Something Fishy in Gore Canyon

Gore Canyon was essential to the route of the Moffat. Anything blocking Gore Canyon would have blocked the Moffat's western march. With nowhere to go, it's doubtful the railroad would have survived.

Apparently, the money and influence of the Rio Grande's owners were the root of many problems that beset the fledgling Moffat. First, a hydroelectric company proposed a dam and reservoir in Gore Canyon. Injunctions flew through the courts. The dam was declared a fraud when it was discovered that the plans

A testament to durable construction, a water tank still sits on the Rollins Pass line of the Moffat. The unusual construction allowed the tank to be insulated in this freezing climate.

lacked a pipe to carry the water to the hydroelectric plant! Next, the U.S. Reclamation Service declared Gore Canyon to be the perfect site for a dam and reservoir. Personal intervention by President Theodore Roosevelt prevented the Reclamation Service from interfering with the Moffat's construction.

The first passenger train chugged through Gore Canyon in 1907. Even if harassment did not directly halt the Moffat's advance, it did slow construction, and the Moffat's finances would get more and more precarious.

Coal, Coal, and More Coal

Trains finally reached the all-important coal fields and then Steamboat Springs. Craig, the western terminus reached in 1911, would be as close as the Moffat's mainline would ever get to the Pacific Ocean.

Rollins Pass

The twenty-three-mile ghost over Rollins Pass might be the most spectacular abandoned railroad location in the world. Why would anyone build a railroad here, miles above timberline, buried in twenty feet of snow for seven months of the year? It was, of course, a temporary expedient. A tunnel bypassing Rollins Pass was proposed for completion in a year or, at most, two. Things didn't go as planned, however, and trains fought the snow on Rollins Pass for almost a quarter century.

As a "temporary" line, Rollins Pass was constructed frugally. Grades were steep, curves tight, and drainage poor. Starting from the eastern approach, three long loops of track called the Giant's Ladder provided a stairway for the straining locomotives. Trainmen could fill the loco's tender with water from the tank at Jenny Lake—if they could stand against the howling winds falling down the mountainous slope to the west. Around the Needle's Eye Tunnel, the tracks hugged a seven-hundred-foot-high cliff. Trains that derailed there were in mortal danger, and crews restored their train's footing carefully lest all crash down the mountainside. The summit station was called Corona, a little city where buildings and railroad track were covered by snowsheds, so they would not be lost for the whole winter. Exhausted locomotives could take water and coal while their human drivers could take food at the restaurant. There was even a hotel with cables stretched over its roof to keep it intact in hundred-mile-per-hour windstorms.

Coming down the west side, the trains circumnavigated a track spiral like the Georgetown Loop, only longer. The lower track of the loop was hidden in a tunnel on top of which the Loop's trestle was stacked like a model train set. Nearer to the western foot of the pass, the busy town of Arrow included a depot, restaurant, stock pens, sawmill, and many saloons, as well as railroad facilities. While once a prosperous location, today you can barely figure out where this community existed.

The men who pushed trains over Rollins faced a Herculean task. Three of the Moffat's rotary snowplows steamed over the pass, but the snow melted in the mountain sunshine during the day and encased the track in ice at night. Men suffered through 40-below temperatures and 100-mph winds. Soaked from crawling under broken locomotives and tired from sixteen-hour days, they'd barely make it to the snowshed at Corona. There, with a shed full of steam locos trapped by a storm, they'd frequently lose consciousness from the noxious fumes. Falling against a steam pipe meant severe burns. Being trapped in the shed when a locomotive crossed meant certain death, as victims would be ground up in its undulating driving rods. When the line was closed for weeks at a time by snow, the men would stay with their marooned trains—even walking to Corona to eat and then returning to groom their iron steeds and wait for the rumble of rescue by a snowplow.

A passenger train climbs through the Needle's Eye Tunnel overlooking the track circling Yankee Doodle Lake below. As with many railroad photos from the early 1900s, the train has been retouched to make it more visible or simply drawn in where no train existed. (Courtesy, Denver Public Library, Western History Collection, MCC-1630. Photo by L. C. McClure.)

It was also in 1911 that David Moffat died in New York City while trying to procure financing to complete his transcontinental railroad. The "temporary" track on Rollins Pass had served seven years as the Moffat's mainline. Financing was desperately needed to build a tunnel to bypass this profit-draining nightmare of a railroad track.

Coal traffic boomed, and the Moffat should have been a profitable railroad. Such was not the case, for the cost of operating trains over Rollins Pass was staggering, especially in winter. Trains were delayed days or even weeks by snow. Who was going to invest in a coal mine that couldn't get its product to market in the winter when demand was highest? A rotary snow plow pushed by five, six, or even seven engines struggled to get only two dozen cars loaded with coal over Rollins Pass.

The cost of locomotives and snow-fighting equipment, the coal burned in the locomotives, the maintenance of those mighty machines, the many crewmen's salaries, and the repairs to the line's "temporary" railroad track through the sky added up to a staggering sum. Rumor had it that additional traffic caused a net loss for the Moffat. Clearly a railway that makes less money when it does more business does not have a future. The usual bankruptcies followed. The road's name was changed from Denver, Northwestern & Pacific to a less pretentious Denver & Salt Lake Railroad. Despite its new name, the Moffat's mainline never got any closer to Salt Lake City, and its losses continued to mount. Something had to be done or the Moffat was doomed.

The Great Tunnel

Something was done. A publicly owned tunnel had been proposed as early as 1911, the year of Moffat's death. Denver wanted a tunnel to divert western slope water to its expanding population and economy.

RAILWAY TO HEAVEN

Chapel cars were churches in railroad cars, complete with organ, hymnals, and living quarters for the minister. American Baptist chapel car "Emmanuel" first crossed Rollins Pass in 1924. One wonders if the Reverend and Mrs. Blanchard sang "Nearer, My God, to Thee" as they approached the 11,600-foot summit. Before the Moffat Tunnel was built, Emmanuel would make two round trips over Rollins Pass to minister to those in need of salvation in Craig and Steamboat Springs. It later traveled through the six-mile bore to minister in Phippsburg and on to Yampa, where it was struck by lightning. Retired in 1942, the railroad car is now displayed at Prairie Village near Madison, South Dakota.

Chapel car Emmanuel, built in 1893, was the second car built by the American Baptist Publication Society. Shown here near the turn of the twentieth century, Emmanuel included everything the minister would need, from a pulpit and organ to a bedroom and kitchen. (Courtesy, American Baptist Historical Society.)

Above: *A pop car, a small, self-propelled vehicle used to carry railroad workers, waits in Glenwood Springs, with the Hotel Colorado peeking through the trees. Although farther along than Moffat trains ran, Glenwood Springs is a frequent destination for travelers on the Amtrak train that starts its journey by following the Moffat route west from Denver.*

Left: *A caved-in tunnel, marked by shards of wood timbers in the foreground, was the beginning of a spiral of track on the Moffat line. Eastbound trains would exit this portal of the tunnel and eventually cross over the trestle in the background. Compare this to the photograph on page 70.*

Above: *A locomotive engineer's heart-stopping view from near the Needle's Eye Tunnel shows the Moffat line far below as it loops around Yankee Doodle Lake. On the left side of the lake, the pile of rocks is evidence of an aborted attempt by the Burlington to build a railroad tunnel under Rollins Pass before the Moffat arrived.*

Facing page: *After traveling the Moffat route from Denver to the Dotsero Cutoff, the Rio Grande Zephyr speeds along near the Colorado River through the depths of Glenwood Canyon in this photograph from 1980. This train has since been replaced by Amtrak's California Zephyr. The idea to build a dome car, a passenger car with a glass dome atop its roof, was born in Glenwood Canyon.*

As injunctions flew in the courts over the disputed Gore Canyon, the railroad flew surveyors over the waters of the Colorado River in that canyon. This survey crew was photographed in the early 1900s. (Courtesy, Denver Public Library, Western History Collection, X-22214.)

Combining the water and railroad tunnels would generate additional support for both projects. A useful water tunnel would have to be lower and much longer than the originally proposed 2.6-mile railroad tunnel. The completed Moffat Tunnel, over 6 miles long through the granite mountain, echoed the pounding hooves of an iron horse in February 1928, as the first regularly scheduled train blasted through.

Once the tunnel was finished, the Moffat resurrected the idea of a connection with the Rio Grande. The Rio Grande itself, which had long opposed the Moffat, would build this connection. Called the Dotsero Cutoff, the line connected Dotsero, east of Glenwood Springs, with Orestod, near Bond. Dotsero was named for the "decimal point zero" that the surveyor marked on his map at the start of the connecting track; and if you haven't figured it out yet, Orestod is Dotsero spelled backwards! The opening of the cutoff was celebrated in Bond in June 1934. The Burlington's transcontinental connection to the West was finally realized, and they rejoiced by sending the Burlington Zephyr, the first diesel streamliner, to remote Bond. Now, trains from Denver crossed the mountains through the Moffat Tunnel, dropped down Gore Canyon, followed the Colorado River along the Dotsero Cutoff, and started their Pacific journey polishing the Rio Grande's rails. The frustrated dreams of William Loveland's Colorado Central, John Evans's South Park, David Moffat's Denver, Northwestern & Pacific, and a generation of Colorado citizens were finally realized. Denver sat proudly astride a transcontinental railroad route.

The Rio Grande, which had so vigorously opposed the Moffat, saw fit to merge with it in 1947. The mainline through the Moffat Tunnel would be destined to become more important to the Rio Grande than its hard-won track through the Royal Gorge over Tennessee Pass.

Exploring: Moffat Tunnel Trains
Amtrak's California Zephyr runs west from Denver following the same route as the legendary Moffat, through the six-mile inky-black Moffat Tunnel, down fought-over Gore Canyon, and alongside the long-delayed Dotsero Cutoff. David Moffat's wonderfully restored private car, "Marcia," is exhibited in Craig.

The route over Rollins Pass is now an unpaved road, but it is often closed to through traffic, requiring excursions from both sides to see the entire line. To get there from Rollinsville on Colorado Highway 119, turn west on an unpaved road, which becomes the old Moffat railroad grade on the eastern approach to Rollins Pass. The western side can be accessed from U.S. Highway 40 near Winter Park.

PART III

HERE, THERE, AND EVERYWHERE

Colorado's mountain railroads are ubiquitous. As you drive through Colorado, you are seldom out of sight of a railroad, either abandoned or existing. At Winter Park, trains explode out of the Moffat Tunnel and head west along U.S. Highway 40. West of Golden, U.S. Highway 6 follows the path of the Colorado Central, Colorado's first mountain railroad. Interstate 70 threads Glen-wood Canyon along with the Rio Grande standard-gauge mainline to Salt Lake. You can still see the tunnels of the Colorado Midland west of Manitou Springs on U.S. Highway 24. In western Colorado, Highway 145 follows the route of the Rio Grande Southern over Lizard Head Pass. Many more railroads and abandoned grades are visible from Colorado's highways.

An amazing number of small towns had passenger railroad service. You could ride the steam cars to Hartsel, Telluride, and Steamboat Springs. Three railroads served Cripple Creek. A trio of railroads also carried passengers to and from Leadville. Four rail lines chugged into the little mountain valley in which Silverton nestles. Because private transportation meant a hazardous days-long trip uncomfortably perched on a saddle or bouncing along in a horse-drawn wagon, it is no wonder that even the smallest mountain hamlet offered public transport on smooth steel rails in comfortable seats warmed by a coal stove.

This part describes some of Colorado's shorter ghost railroads, improbably linking many small towns along the Crystal and Purgatoire River valleys with the outside world. It continues with the trolleys that ran through many of Colorado's cities, including Fort Collins, and concludes with another improbable line—one over which a railroad war was fought—the Rio Grande, which still runs through the bottom of the Royal Gorge.

Streamlined passenger locomotives marked the end of an era in which railroads were the primary mode of transportation in the United States. Canon City & Royal Gorge locomotives are painted much like those of the Rio Grande in the 1950s.

CHAPTER 7

GHOST RAILWAYS

The Trains of the Crystal and Purgatoire River Valleys

Colorado's abandoned railroad specters include the little narrow-gauge coal cars of the Book Cliff Railway, north of Grand Junction, and the precious-metal trains of the Colorado & Northwestern Railway, west

of Boulder. Trains also moved logs from the woods to buzzing sawmills especially around Dolores and Pagosa Springs. The Uintah Railway carried gilsonite through the high desert country northwest of Grand Junction. The mountain-ringed San Luis Valley is the unlikely location of two agricultural railways, the San Luis Central Railroad and the San Luis Valley Southern Railway.

John Osgood, born in Brooklyn, New York, was a self-made man. He fathered Colorado Fuel & Iron, operator of a huge steel mill in Pueblo, Colorado. In order to supply his

steel mill, he needed to build railroads. Some of his railroads carried coal and coke from both the Purgatoire River and Crystal River valleys. The coking process removes moisture and impurities from coal. What remains, called coke, is almost pure carbon and burns cleanly with intense heat.

Rails That Time Forgot

The Purgatoire River rises toward the snow-capped Culebra Range west of Trinidad. It's a quiet, peaceful valley today but such was not always the case. Residues of the past are everywhere. The weedy railroad track, the vestiges of miniature metropolises, the battered bricks of coke ovens, and the black mounds that mark entrances to old coal mines are all clues to what happened in this valley.

Facing page: Construction of the Allen Mine in 1951 required an almost ten-mile extension of the Colorado & Wyoming. This unit train is being loaded with coal as it moves through the silo.

Inset: Coke-oven ruins at Cokedale mark a well-preserved coal-mining town. A one-mile-long Rio Grande branch connecting with the Colorado & Wyoming served Cokedale, as did the Trinidad Electric Railway, whose trolleys carried residents between the town and Trinidad.

Ruins of coke ovens are precious little reminders of the once-thriving community of Tercio. The mining company built 151 homes, a huge company store, a school, and a social club, all at almost eight thousand feet above sea level. Passenger trains served Tercio, coming and going twice each day.

In late 1900, Colorado Fuel & Iron built a standard-gauge railroad, the Southern Division of the Colorado & Wyoming Railway, to carry coal. Not all coal would be shipped in its original form on the Colorado & Wyoming. As quickly as mines at Valdez and Primero made coal available, it was converted to coke at the huge ovens in Segundo. Trains carried the coke to Pueblo to make steel.

Those who rode the train from Trinidad to Segundo could listen to the voices of some of its other passengers, new miners fresh from the Old World, and hear Spanish, Italian, and a half dozen other languages. The Colorado & Wyoming's passenger train was called the "Spaghetti Flyer" because of all those Italian voices. Hundreds of immigrants and their families sought their fortunes in the coal mines of southern Colorado. During the day, smoke from the coke ovens muted the sun. At night, the ovens' red glow challenged the darkness. Always, there was noise—the chugging of locomotives tugging stubborn coal cars, the squealing of railroad car wheels sliding around sharp curves, the whirring of the machinery of the industrial revolution.

The railroad was extended down the south fork of the Purgatoire to reach Tercio by March 1902. By April, coal was already being mined there. Mines were also poked into the earth at Cuatro, Quinto, and Sexto. Company towns were built. Homes, company stores, libraries, and schools lined the valley. An annual picnic train became the high point of the valley for school children. Two mine rescue cars delivered emergency equipment to the mouths of mines when disaster struck. Disaster did sometimes strike, and the valley had more than its share of widows and orphans.

Between 1901 and 1908, Colorado Fuel & Iron established seven coal mines along the river, anticipating the sale of coal to railroads and coke to smelters. All this optimistic construction was a mistake, however. As the twentieth century dawned, the precious-metal mines of Colorado started their long, slow slide to oblivion. Smelters cut back production, or closed completely, and the demand for coke never met expectations. The need for coal to power engines pulling trains to Colorado's dying mining camps also declined. To add to the woes of the valley, labor strife surfaced in the strikes of 1903 and 1913. World War I brought a short-lived surge in demand, but it was not enough to save the industry.

Most of Pueblo's steel had gone to manufacture railroad rails. As the Great Depression settled over the country, many railroad lines were torn up, causing Pueblo's production of new rail to cease. By the 1930s, most of the mines in the Purgatoire valley were closed. Tercio survived for three decades after mining ended, but it was never the same. A brief attempt at agriculture saw trains hauling lettuce to market;

The Trinidad Dam flooded the original Colorado & Wyoming line near the river. A ten-mile relocation circumvented the Trinidad Reservoir and took trains though this one-hundred-foot-deep cut.

timber and livestock were also shipped. It was a far cry from the favorable first years of the century, but the railroad did survive—barely.

World War II caused a resurgence of demand for coal, and the railroad prospered. In 1951, the track to Tercio down the south fork of the Purgatoire was removed, due to a decline in coal traffic. Postwar consumer demand for automobiles and appliances was booming, however, and the Colorado & Wyoming was extended westward down the north fork to the new Allen Mine near Stonewall. Eventually, the Maxwell Mine was also developed nearby. Starting in 1971, unit trains of coal began to drop down the valley. These unit trains, which are trains that remain assembled in a single unit, were loaded as they moved through a silo and then routed directly to the Pueblo steel mill without any intermediate switching of cars. The future looked bright for both the coal mines and the Colorado & Wyoming, but mining would come full circle yet again. In the last decades of the twentieth century, the mines closed, the sounds of trains no longer echoed off the hills, and the valley returned yet again to peaceful slumber in the shadow of the Culebra Range.

Coal along the Crystal

The Crystal River valley, south of Carbondale, is flanked by the Elk Mountains. In less than forty miles, almost every variant of Colorado mountain railroading was once represented. There were railroads projected but never started; railroads graded but on which rail was never laid; a railroad that ran only a single train; standard-gauge and narrow-gauge railroads; railroads with conventional and geared steam locomotives; an electrically powered railroad; a railroad that included "and San Juan" in its name but never got there; steep winding high railroads; railroads that snaked over switchbacks; and railroads that undulated around hairpin loops of track.

Coal and marble deposits encouraged railroad schemers to tap the Crystal River country as early as the 1880s. Paper railroads were created in the minds of entrepreneurs but were never built. Miles of grade were expensively constructed, but steel was never laid on them. The Aspen & Western Railway completed a thirteen-mile line to a coal mine. Unfortunately,

In 1931, this marble monolith made a four-day trip, at less than a mile a day, down the Yule Tram to be transferred to the Crystal River & San Juan, shown here. Imagine the tension as this magnificent block, the largest block of marble ever quarried, was lowered down the mountainside by two little electric locomotives. One misstep and it would crash down to the valley below. Its fifty-six tons would eventually become the Tomb of the Unknown Soldier. (Courtesy, Denver Public Library, Western History Collection, X-12283.)

the original survey of the coal seam was faulty. With a clearly inadequate coal supply, the narrow-gauge line hauled only one trainload of coal, and did that with a leased locomotive.

With the worst timing possible, Colorado Fuel & Iron began construction of the Crystal River Railway in 1893 but promptly shut it down with the Silver Panic of that year. Operations began again in 1899. Twenty miles of standard-gauge track served the coal mines at Placita and the coke ovens at Redstone. An eleven-mile narrow-gauge branch—a continuous string of steep hairpin loops—served coal mines at Coalbasin. Railroad passengers traveling through Carbondale continued their journey on narrow-gauge cars to Coalbasin where another company town housed the men that actually mined the coal. The Coalbasin turntable had to be covered with a

round shed to allow its use in the snowy winters, and a narrow-gauge rotary snowplow was stationed there to begin its downhill struggle to Redstone. If snow removal was needed on the standard-gauge line to Carbondale, the wheels on the plow would be changed at Redstone.

Like the towns of the Purgatoire valley, Redstone was a well-built company town. In addition to homes and the coke plant, the town had extensive railroad facilities where the standard-gauge and narrow-gauge trains met. A school educated the children of employees. A company store provided the necessities of life. A club with a library and poolroom offered activities. A town band entertained. Outlawing liquor in mining camps had not always had the desired effect, so a different strategy was tried at the Redstone and Coalbasin clubs. Alcohol was served, but no man could buy a drink for another. Without the cry of "this round is on me," the endless parade of men reciprocating the favor was avoided, as well as many morning-after headaches.

John Osgood, the man responsible for all this development, enjoyed Cleveholm, a spectacular mansion built here in the remote wilds of Colorado. His private railroad car would be staffed and parked near his palatial home for trips to conduct business outside the isolated Crystal River valley.

Marble Monuments

Yet another entrepreneur, Colonel Channing Meek, began developing the marble deposits farther south in the valley. Connecting with the Crystal River Railway at Placita, Crystal River & San Juan Railway trains hurried along seven miles to the town of Marble and the finishing mill that Meek erected there. The town grew as marble became a major export. Although associated with expensive, elegant construction in most of the world, low-grade marble was a sturdy and inexpensive building material in the Crystal River valley.

The supports for the mill's traveling crane were built of it. The engines of the Crystal River & San Juan spun around on a turntable in a white hollow—the only turntable pit in the world lined with marble. Marble rubble was dumped along the riverbank to prevent erosion, and an immense marble wall protected the mill and town from avalanches that regularly sped down the mountainside. By the end of 1910, Colorado Fuel & Iron had given up on the Coalbasin mines, the coke plant at Redstone, and the Crystal River itself. The Crystal River & San Juan now took control of the entire thirty-mile track from Marble to Carbondale.

At its farthest extent, the marble finishing mill and railroad complex were about a half mile long. The electrically operated Yule Creek Railway, commonly

A rusted conveyor protrudes from a small marble building. Although the mill included machinery for moving, cutting, and polishing marble, much of the delicate shaping was handwork performed by armies of skilled artisans.

A Yule Tram train prepares to leave the quarry station with a trainload of marble in this photograph circa 1912. What appears to be a flatcar with a small hut on either end is actually one of two electric locomotives on the four-mile-long railway. (Courtesy, Denver Public Library, Western History Collection, GB-8456. Photo by G. L. Beam.)

called the Yule Tram, connected the quarry to the mill. The Yule Tram traveled up and down grades as steep as 17 percent, normally the province of cog railroads and mountain goats. Operation was possible only because the electric locomotives had better traction uphill than steam locos, and because the loaded marble trains were helped downhill by gravity. Gravity's assistance was not always welcome, and many runaway trains caused injury and death. Colonel Meek, himself, died as a result of injuries suffered when jumping from a runaway Yule Tram train in 1912.

Perhaps not coincidentally, marble production also peaked in 1912. Another quarry, the Strauss Quarry, opened across Yule Creek from the original Colorado Yule Quarry in 1910. The new quarry was served by a switchback railroad that owned only one geared steam locomotive for the steep climb. By 1915, the Strauss Quarry and its Treasury Mountain Railroad had closed for good.

Marble-hauling trains chugged up the valley through good and bad times, as marble became more fashionable or less fashionable for construction. In addition to marble, trains in the area moved coal from the Placita Mine, livestock, and agricultural products. In 1914, marble from the Colorado Yule Quarry was chosen for the Lincoln Memorial in Washington, D.C. Train after train of marble crept down the mountain from quarry to mill. Finished marble pieces for the Lincoln Memorial meandered down the rail line to Carbondale for shipment east on the Rio Grande.

Huge marble blocks continued to be hoisted onto the flat cars of the Yule Tram until 1941. In that year, the mill machinery was sold and moved out on the Crystal River & San Juan. Everything was dismantled, and quiet descended on the Crystal River valley after over half a century of industrial development.

Exploring: Coal Black and Marble White

Most of the railroad track that was once the Colorado & Wyoming mainline west from Trinidad to the Allen Mine was removed in 2003. Don't miss Trinidad's historic downtown of substantial buildings and its rich Hispanic heritage—a heritage much older than the coal mines. Drive Colorado Highway 12 west from Trinidad to follow the railroad. There are ruins of coke ovens at Cokedale, considered one of the West's best-preserved coal-mining camps. Many other coal-mining villages still exist, including Segundo. An unpaved road leads from just east of Stonewall south to the site of Tercio. There the company store stands in a field, and ruins of coke ovens line a hillside.

Visit both Redstone and Marble. See the Redstone Inn, a building that once housed unmarried employees. Osgood's mansion, Cleveholm, stands majestically just south of Redstone, and in some years, tours are offered. The remains of the coke ovens are visible along Colorado Highway 133. At Marble, explore the mill site where there are marble walls and supports for the traveling crane. You can spot the turntable pit, but the marble lining is gone. North of the mill, along the railroad grade, you can find the place where defective marble pieces were discarded. The Yule Tram grade is now an unpaved road, but public travel is discouraged due to marble-carrying trucks and natural hazards.

CHAPTER 8

Clang Went the Trolley

Streetcars and Interurban Railways

Before automobiles became a practical mode of personal mobility, public transit was essential to most sizable cities. Streetcars strolled the avenues, first powered by horses or mules, and later by electricity. Electrically powered interurban railways also connected one town to another. Almost everyone called street and interurban railways "trolleys" and recognized the clang of the trolley's bell.

In 1871, Denver's horsecars were the first city rail transit in Colorado. Denver had an extensive system of cable cars that was replaced by the ubiquitous electric trolley. You could ride the trolley from Colorado Springs right to the Cog depot in Manitou Springs to continue to the summit of Pikes Peak. It's no surprise that the large cities of Pueblo and Colorado Springs offered trolley transportation to their citizens, but it is surprising that residents of smaller cities like Greeley, Boulder, Grand Junction, and Trinidad also heard the clang of the trolley's bell. The Trinidad Electric Railway not only included streetcars but also an interurban railway that served the coal camps nearby. Passengers stepping off the steam cars of the Rio Grande in little Durango must have been surprised to see a trolley waiting for them at the depot. Even two-mile-high Leadville tried horsecars for a time, but snow and icy conditions made operation next to impossible in winter. Many towns were served by the interurban trains on two lines between Cripple Creek and Victor.

Facing page: The trolley pole forces a small wheel against the overhead wire, which collects electricity to operate the car. The fare for the Fort Collins Municipal Railway was still just a nickel in the late 1940s.

Inset: Denver's first public rail transport was a horsecar. The horse would pull the car uphill and then ride the car as it coasted downhill, as shown in this 1903 photo. (Courtesy, Denver Public Library, Western History Collection, X-6890. Photo by W. M. Flanders.)

One of those towns, Midway, was the highest trolley stop in the nation at an altitude of 10,487 feet.

The first automobile arrived in Durango in 1902, carried on a narrow-gauge steam train. It was a portent of things to come. Automobiles became less expensive and more reliable. More people bought autos and demanded better-quality roads. The trolley's losses would mount, and trolley lines, both big and small, slowly succumbed.

Clanging Once Again

Small Denver & Interurban Railroad trolleys wobbled down the Fort Collins streets from 1908 until 1951. Dad would ride the trolley to work at the Great Western Sugar Plant. Mom would take the kids to play at City Park. Grandma rode the little streetcars to Grandview Cemetery to visit Grandpa's grave. The little kids rode the cars to grammar school, and one of the older children caught the car to attend classes at Colorado A&M College. The whole family enjoyed an outing to the Lake Lindenmeier resort on Sunday. The Denver & Interurban trolley line folded, without warning, in the middle of the night in 1918. City life was devastated. An election to allow the city to buy the trolley line was passed by a landslide, and the electric cars became the Fort Collins Municipal Railway in 1919. Fares were the lowest in the nation, and service was extraordinary for a small city. After World War II, however, red ink began to flow into the ledger, and the electric motors whirred to a halt in 1951. The idea to restore the last remaining trolley first surfaced in 1976. Soon thereafter, citizens suggested that track be laid to allow the little car to travel down Mountain Avenue. With an incredible all-volunteer effort, trolley car 21 was restored and track relaid down Mountain Avenue. The little car ran again in 1984. By 1986, you could, once again, ride the trolley from near downtown all the way to City Park.

Exploring: The Fort Collins Municipal Railway and the Platte Valley Trolley

On some days, Fort Collins's restored trolley trundles up and down Mountain Avenue, just west of downtown. Trolley restorations are also in progress in Colorado Springs at the old Rock Island roundhouse on Steele Drive. The Platte Valley Trolley runs near the Denver Children's Museum. Coming full circle, Denver is now diligently building light rail lines and trains, modern descendants of trolley cars.

Above: The squeal of steel trolley wheels rounding a curve was once a common sound in U.S. cities. After the City of Fort Collins bought the trolley system, they purchased small four-wheeled cars like this one, called Birney cars. Birneys were mass produced to a standardized design and could be operated by one person.

Left: It was not unusual for trolley companies to build their own cars since they were constructed easily from wood using readily available technology. The trucks (wheels and motors) and electrical equipment would be purchased. Around 1910, employees of the Denver Tramway Company still have much work to complete on this trolley. (Courtesy, Denver Public Library, Western History Collection, X-18378.)

Facing page: Deep snow halts trolleys on Denver's Lawrence Street in 1913. (Courtesy, Denver Public Library, Western History Collection, X-28955.)

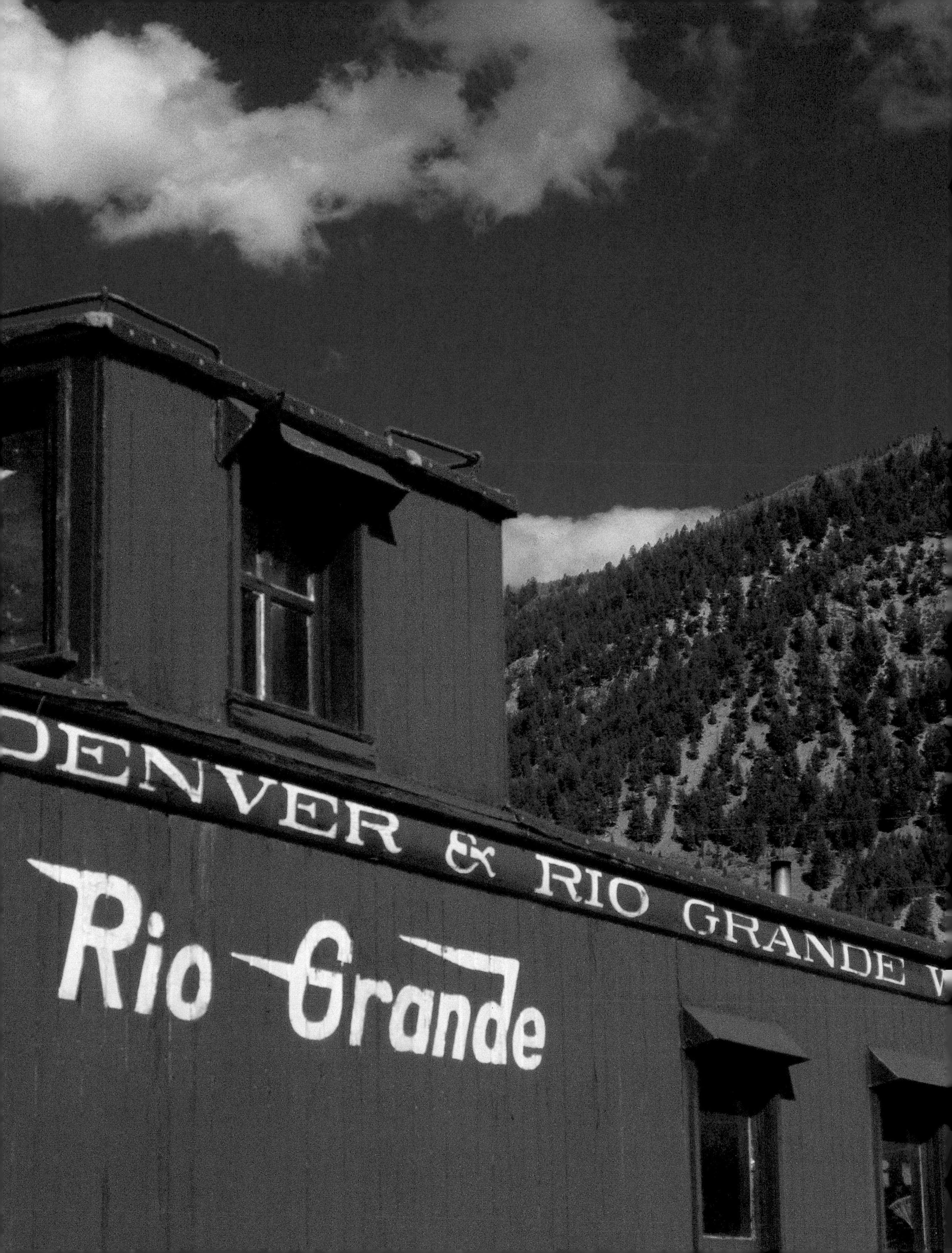
DENVER & RIO GRANDE W
Rio Grande

THE GIANT BABY RAILROAD
The Denver & Rio Grande Railway

The greatest narrow-gauge empire was unquestionably the Denver & Rio Grande, founded by General William Jackson Palmer. Philadelphia-born Palmer had been educated in England, where he witnessed the battle of the gauges between advocates of standard gauge (4 feet 8½ inches) and wide gauge (7 feet ¼ inch) tracks. Palmer had also been a Union officer in the American Civil War and the chief construction engineer for the Kansas Pacific on its march across the Great Plains to Denver. As he formulated his plan for the Rio Grande, advocates of narrow-gauge track preached their sermon to any who would listen. With limited capital, Palmer made the practical decision to space his rails only three feet apart, taking advantage of lower construction costs. Costs were destined to be considerable, for the words "Rio Grande" in the corporate title were a reference to the

Rio Grande River on the Mexican border. Called the "baby railroad" because its first locomotives were so tiny, the toddler was expected to crawl all the way to Mexico City! Its tracks started south from Denver in 1870 and in 1871 reached what would become Colorado Springs. Palmer founded the city of Colorado Springs and made his home there among the red rocks.

A Rat on the Pass

Raton Pass, the "Pass of the Rat," is the only practical rail route south from Trinidad. Trapper, soldier, saloon keeper, and mountain man "Uncle Dick" Wooten operated the toll road over Raton. In the late 1870s, both the Santa Fe and the Rio Grande coveted this location. With room for only a single practical railroad, the first to start construction would own the route and the other would be

Facing page: This Rio Grande caboose, now resting in Lake City, once traveled the railroad's entire narrow-gauge empire.

Inset: The Santa Fe won initial possession of the Royal Gorge, but the Rio Grande had possession of the rest of the route to Leadville—including this section of Brown's Canyon on the Arkansas River, now a popular destination for rafting.

left wondering where to go next. The two railroads deviously tapped each other's telegraph lines and deciphered their secret codes. The Santa Fe learned that the Rio Grande was about to make its move at dawn: A Rio Grande construction crew was to start work and claim the route.

But there was a rat on the Pass—a Santa Fe agent who had quietly become a drinking buddy of Uncle Dick. After revealing his true identity, the agent convinced Uncle Dick to support the Santa Fe's claim to the route. In the dead of night, before the Rio Grande's crew arrived, the Santa Fe started construction. Legend has it that the Santa Fe's construction crew was actually composed of Uncle Dick's circle of barroom buddies. By the end of 1878, Santa Fe trains traversed the Pass of the Rat.

Thus, what might have been was not to be. The Rio Grande's diminutive trains would never whistle into Mexico City, and the Santa Fe would build its tracks to the Pacific. The Rio Grande had already begun to realize its true destiny when its trains climbed west over Veta Pass the year before the skirmish at Raton, however. It would become the king of Colorado's mountain railroads.

The War in the Abyss

Just after the controversy at Raton, a full-fledged war erupted between the Rio Grande and the Santa Fe

After mountain man "Uncle Dick" Wooten helped beat the Rio Grande to a route over Raton Pass, the grateful Santa Fe named a locomotive after him. It is pictured here in a photograph from 1919. (Courtesy, Denver Public Library, Western History Collection, OP-662. Photo by O. C. Perry.)

Above: *A Canon City & Royal Gorge train prepares to depart for the precipitous depths for which it is named.*

Left: *The Royal Gorge Bridge, over a thousand feet above the railroad, leaps the chasm.*

RAILS TO CARRY IRON

It's dark, cold, and snowy. A train of heavy iron ore picks up speed drifting down the steep hill. The locomotive engineer whistles for brakes, and brakemen climb to the tops of the swaying cars. Using wooden clubs for leverage, they wind down the brakewheel on one car and then run to the next to apply more brakes.

It was in this way that almost a quarter-million tons of iron ore began a journey from the Calumet mine to the great steel mill at Pueblo. Just north of Salida along the Tennessee Pass line of the Rio Grande, a seven-mile branch of track once plunged into the hills east of the Arkansas River. Iron deposits were discovered at Calumet in the 1870s. Narrow-gauge track reached the iron mine in 1881, and trains began their battle with the incredibly steep 8 percent gradients.

As the mines were dug deeper, the ore changed character, becoming difficult to use to make steel. When the mines reached water in 1889, it wasn't worth the expense of pumping. An occasional train struggled up the branch until 1908 to serve a marble quarry. Biblical floods roared through the canyon after the last ore train coasted down the line, carrying away two-and-a-half miles of rail. The remaining rails rusted and ties rotted until 1923 when the branch was finally removed.

Right: The center pivot of a narrow-gauge turntable rests amid the fall color near the Calumet iron mine. The turntable was removed after it was determined that it was safer to operate the steep branch with the locomotive always facing uphill below the train— exactly like Manitou & Pike's Peak cog steam locomotives are operated on its steep track.

Below: The lower part of the Rio Grande's Calumet Branch was bottled up between rock walls. Farther uphill, marble was quarried and transported down the branch.

over the "Grand Canyon" of the Arkansas River, the Royal Gorge. Just west of Canon City, the Arkansas rushed through a rocky parting of the earth. At one point, the canyon floor descended one thousand feet below the rim, and its walls crowded the river into a chute just thirty feet across. Clearly, it would be difficult to build a railroad there and impossible to build two tracks. Both the Santa Fe and the Rio Grande eyed the route up the Royal Gorge as the easiest way to reach the rich Leadville silver boom. If the Santa Fe occupied the Gorge, the Rio Grande would literally have nowhere to go. Its southern route to Mexico City had already been truncated, and its western advance across the mountains would be severely limited. More importantly, the Santa Fe's standard-gauge trains would be formidable competition for the Rio Grande's narrow gauge—and the Santa Fe threatened to parallel all the Rio Grande's lines with competing standard-gauge tracks. Rival construction crews met in the narrow canyon. Strange accidents began to befall each other's work parties. Lawsuits and countersuits flew in the courts. The Santa Fe's claim to the Royal Gorge was upheld, but the Rio Grande occupied the route farther ahead between the gorge and Leadville. An armed band of Rio Grande toughs held down a stone fort and prevented the Santa Fe from building to Leadville. The Santa Fe contracted western legend Bat Masterson to arrive at Pueblo with a hundred gunslingers to scare the Rio Grande into submission. Although a few men were killed, most of the war was a bluff. A settlement was eventually made that would have long-term consequences: The Santa Fe agreed to halt its westward advance through Colorado, and its rail line through the Royal Gorge became part of the Rio Grande. In exchange, the Rio Grande agreed not to compete to the south where the Santa Fe would make its way to the Pacific.

For many years, passenger trains transiting the Royal Gorge included an open-air car from which passengers could thrill to the thousand-foot-deep gash. The last Rio Grande passenger train passed through the Royal Gorge in 1967. Starting in 1999, passenger trains of the Canon City & Royal Gorge Railroad glided through these depths, and visitors riding in open-air cars again craned their necks to view the rocky ramparts.

The Santa Fe actually built the famous Hanging Bridge at the bottom of the Royal Gorge. The railroad was hung from steel beams anchored in the rock walls above the tracks.

In this photo taken on February 27, 1910, the Chicago White Sox baseball team poses with a Rio Grande locomotive on Hanging Bridge at the narrowest part of the Royal Gorge. (Courtesy, Denver Public Library, Western History Collection, GB-7443. Photo by G. L. Beam.)

Above: *An eastbound Rio Grande train rolls into Pando on the western approach to the summit of Tennessee Pass.*

Left: *The Canon City & Royal Gorge offers cab rides. For an extra charge, visitors can ride in a locomotive whose appearance is strongly associated with the streamlined era of rail passenger travel.*

RAILS TO CARRY LIMESTONE

Until 1984, travelers on U.S. Highway 50 encountered several unusually placed railroad crossings still in use on Monarch Pass. The route at Garfield was especially puzzling, with the tracks cutting across the highway at a steep angle. This Rio Grande branch was the last operating switchback railroad in Colorado. Trains loaded with limestone and bound for the Pueblo steel mill left the quarry at Monarch, rolling up and down one switchback after another like some huge slow-motion pinball machine built on the mountainside.

Rio Grande narrow-gauge trains reached the ten-thousand-foot-high Monarch Quarry in 1883, sixteen miles west of Salida. When the narrow-gauge line over Marshall Pass was removed, the narrow track to Monarch was doomed. All the narrow-gauge steam-locomotive servicing facilities were removed from Salida and concentrated in Alamosa. Diesel locomotives on standard-gauge rails replaced the narrow-gauge tracks in 1956, but today, even those wider tracks are just a memory. On the eastern approach to the summit of Monarch Pass,

however, you can still find places where the railroad once crossed U.S. 50, and you will have no trouble finding the huge limestone quarry.

Narrow-gauge steam trains had last climbed Monarch Pass in 1956, but Rio Grande diesel-powered trains still zig-zagged down the switchbacks on this cool autumn day in 1980.

A freight train trundles along a placid portion of the Colorado River in Glenwood Canyon.

Tennessee Pass Is Not in Tennessee

Freed from interference, the Rio Grande moved west up the Arkansas River to beat the South Park and the Colorado Midland to Leadville. The Rio Grande's ambitions did not end there. Rails were pushed northwest over Tennessee Pass and on to Aspen and Glenwood Springs. With the competition of the Colorado Midland's standard-gauge tracks breathing down its neck, the Rio Grande began the long process of conversion to standard gauge. The rails over Tennessee Pass had originally been three feet apart, but a tunnel built in 1890 through the summit of the pass signaled the start of conversion to the wider gauge. To provide uninterrupted service, special track allowed both narrow-gauge and standard-gauge trains to travel the same route. Much of the Rio Grande would sport three railroad rails to carry both kinds of trains for years, as late as the early 1970s.

In 1883, the Rio Grande's rails over Marshall Pass had created a narrow-gauge "transcontinental" route, which afforded a three-foot-wide rail path between Denver and Ogden, Utah. What an adventure it must have been to travel from Denver to Ogden on a tiny narrow-gauge steam train. This route was not to last, however. The Tennessee Pass line was instead pushed westward all the way to Ogden as a standard-gauge railroad, and the narrow-gauge track was lopped off west of Montrose. The Marshall Pass line would survive until the mid 1950s as part of the famous Narrow Gauge Circle, the last bastion of Colorado's narrow-gauge trains. The Dotsero Cutoff and the tracks of the Moffat eventually shortened the standard-gauge route, bypassing Tennessee Pass. As this is being written, Tennessee Pass, the highest mainline railroad in the United States, is closed, and its eventual disposition is unknown.

Exploring: The Canon City and Royal Gorge Railroad

North of Leadville, U.S. Highway 24, along with railroad track, crests Tennessee Pass. Traveling along this highway east to Colorado Springs, you'll find Rio Grande locomotive 168 on display in a park near the corner of Sierra Madre Street and Pikes Peak Avenue. Across the street stands the depot that served the Rio Grande and Rock Island. This locomotive and her sister, which is displayed in Alamosa, are the smallest Rio Grande steam engines in existence, although they are considerably bigger than the railroad's first tiny twelve-ton locos. The Rio Grande Scenic Railroad runs passenger trains between Alamosa and the town of LaVeta. Continue southwest to Canon City where you must ride the Canon City & Royal Gorge and explore the town's many museums and a downtown awash with historic structures. On Interstate 25, south of Trinidad, you'll frequently be within sight of the Raton Pass line of the Santa Fe. This is coal-mining country, with remnants of mines and mining hamlets along the way.

PART IV

PINT-SIZED TRAINS IN GALLON-SIZED SCENERY

The words "narrow gauge" quicken the pulse of railroad buffs everywhere. Why? Gauge is simply the distance between the two rails that make up railroad track. After the Civil War, most U.S. railroads standardized this distance at 4 feet 8½ inches, a dimension copied from the spacing of Roman chariot wheels and popular in many countries. A national "standard gauge" allows all railroad cars to run on the tracks of any railroad, but despite this benefit to commerce, a narrow-gauge railroad could be built less expensively and profit where a wider railroad could not.

In Colorado, three-foot-wide narrow-gauge railroads were built to many new destinations. A difference of 1 foot 8½ inches may not seem large until multiplied by the several-hundred-mile length of a railroad. Especially in the mountains, a narrower track meant there was much less dirt to move and rock to blast. Fewer trees were felled to supply the hundreds of thousands of wooden crossties holding the rails apart. Locomotives and cars were smaller and less expensive as well. The apparent fragility of these diminutive trains lost in the mountain vastness highlights the challenges faced by early railroaders and is one of the reasons railroad enthusiasts are so intrigued by Colorado's narrow-gauge railroads.

Traffic increased on some narrow-gauge routes beyond expectations, and standard-gauge railroads, the Moffat and the Colorado Midland, built into the mountains. The Rio Grande had no choice but to widen its narrow-gauge rail lines to standard gauge in order to remain economically competitive. Many narrow-gauge lines saw declining traffic, so there was no point for this expensive gauge conversion. As traffic further declined, even the narrow tracks became impossible money-losers and were torn up. This part explores the Rio Grande narrow-gauge mainlines and four of the many little railroads with which it connected.

Two trains of the Durango & Silverton pass near the Silverton depot.

CHAPTER 10

Exploring the River of Lost Souls

The Narrow-Gauge Circle

By one measure, the Rio Grande's narrow-gauge empire reached its zenith in 1890. Tiny locomotives scurried over eighteen hundred miles of track. Narrow-gauge trains could travel from Denver south to Trinidad, southwest to Durango, and west to Salt Lake City. Although three feet between rails was considered narrow gauge in most of the United States, it had become the de-facto standard of the Colorado mountains. It's no wonder other mountain railroads chose to follow the Rio Grande's lead and enable their trains to directly connect with its vast network of three-foot-gauge track.

The Narrow-Gauge Circle

With the settlement of the "Royal Gorge War," the Rio Grande quickly reached Salida. There the tracks would split. The line for Tennessee Pass struck out to the north, while the track west crested Marshall Pass. Both lines would eventually reach Salt Lake City. Trains on the former arrived on practical standard-gauge track, while trains on the latter would arrive on narrow-gauge rails, a technology destined to decline.

The tentacles of the Rio Grande's narrow-gauge track quickly encircled the southwestern mountains. One route sprouted from Salida, the other from Alamosa. Rails west of Salida reached Gunnison by 1881, the same year that rails from Alamosa reached Durango. By 1882, rails continued west from Gunnison to Grand Junction, while rails north of Durango reached Silverton. A branch line south from Montrose to Ridgway and Ouray was completed in 1887. The track west from Salida bordered the southwestern mountains to the north, while the line west from Alamosa bordered the south. In 1890, a connecting link was forged between Salida and Alamosa as the rails over Poncha Pass were completed. A

Facing page: Passengers on the Narrow-Gauge Circle rode behind locomotives smaller than this Rio Grande loco, which is on display near Cimarron.

Inset: A rickety trestle still stands where the sounds of Creede's saloons once rang up the canyon.

complete circle of narrow-gauge track was formed in 1891 when another railroad, the Rio Grande Southern, bridged the gap between Ridgway and Durango. The mountains were surrounded.

This configuration of railroad routes, known as the Narrow-Gauge Circle, provided the opportunity to promote a special excursion routing. The brave eastern passenger arrived in Denver and changed trains for Salida where the first evening was spent. Boarding a narrow-gauge train early the following morning, the traveler headed west over Marshall Pass, waved at the children of Gunnison, thrilled to the Black Canyon's sheer rock walls, and arrived in Ridgway for the night. The third day saw our adventurer board a new railroad. The Rio Grande Southern crested Lizard Head Pass and edged its way across one precipitous trestle after another. An excited and exhausted passenger slept soundly in Durango that third evening. On the fourth day, our excursionist

again boarded a Rio Grande train, traveling east from Durango over Cumbres Pass to Alamosa and over Poncha Pass to return to Salida. If our friend had enough energy left, a night train provided transportation back to Denver.

The lucky visitor with time to explore the mountains could easily do so. Tickets were valid for sixty days between May 1 and October 31 with unlimited stopovers. From Gunnison, the adventurer might take the train north to the mining camp of Crested Butte or south to Lake City. A horseback ride northeast from Montrose would put him or her on the rim of the deepest part of the Black Canyon of the Gunnison River—twenty-seven hundred feet from rim to river. The delights of the boisterous mining camp of Telluride entertained for a few days. A glimpse of the long ago could be seen at Mesa Verde's ancient cliff dwellings, southwest of Durango. Trains would also take the vacationer west from Alamosa to the rowdy

No Night in Creede

Silver was discovered northwest of Alamosa in 1890. By 1891, a Rio Grande narrow-gauge locomotive poked its head into the nearby town of Creede. Mines and mills dotted West Willow Creek Canyon north of town, and their ruins decorate the canyon's walls to this day, some spectacularly perched on the canyon's rim. The last mine closed in 1985 and passenger trains are again running from South Fork along the Rio Grande River to a point near Creede. In a state known for wild mining camps, Creede was acknowledged as one of the wildest—wide open day and night. Among the crooks who preyed on the hard-working miners of Creede was Mr. Soapy

Smith. Soapy soon outstayed his welcome and left for another gold rush, the Klondike in the Yukon of Canada. Soapy's criminal career ended when he was shot to death in Skagway, Alaska. Both Soapy and the Rio Grande have a connection to that Alaskan village. Many of the Rio Grande's narrow-gauge cars and locomotives went north to Skagway, and some are there to this day on the White Pass & Yukon Route, a narrow-gauge railroad that still carries passengers from tidewater toward the Yukon gold fields. I suppose these Rio Grande narrow-gauge locomotives actually did reach the Pacific Ocean.

Mine buildings perch on the cliffsides west of Creede. The ghost town of Bachelor, home to many miners, sleeps not far from this mine.

Left: Morrow Point Reservoir now covers the Rio Grande's Black Canyon mainline, but a boat tour recreates the experience of traveling along the train's route.

Below: Pictured in the 1880s, the passengers on this Rio Grande train climbing Marshall Pass could expect to go all the way to Salt Lake City on the narrow gauge. At Mears Junction in the valley below, trains from Salida chose to go south over Poncha Pass or west over Marshall Pass. (Courtesy, Colorado Historical Society, CHS-J2175. Photo by W. H. Jackson.)

Right: Courageous brakemen once ran over the tops of railroad cars, tightening brake wheels like this one by using a wooden club inserted in its spokes for leverage. Although modern airbrakes have been used on trains to Silverton for decades, these vestiges of nineteenth-century technology remain on the cars of Colorado's preserved railways and museums.

Below: Passengers will soon begin exploring Silverton as the train nears the fascinating mining town.

Above: Everyone who came to Silverton—from miners to madams—came through the Silverton Depot. It now houses an excellent railroad museum.

Top: You can spot four trains in this photo of Silverton. Hint: One of them is partially hidden among the buildings.

mining camp of Creede. Imagine having the holiday time to spend two months exploring southwestern Colorado and chugging from town to town at a leisurely pace in a comfortable railroad car. What a pleasure it must have been to see beautiful places still barely touched by the hand of man.

The Circle was Broken

The takeover of railroads by the U.S. government during World War I greatly affected the Narrow-Gauge Circle, and the special excursion routing was dropped, never to be restored. Amazingly, the circle of track was not broken until 1948 when the rails through the Black Canyon were taken up. Little by little, the great orbit around the mountains was dismantled. By 1956, rails over Marshall Pass were hauled away, and Salida would no longer experience the sounds and smells of steam locomotives. All the narrow-gauge equipment was moved to fortress Alamosa, where the tiny trains would make their last stand against progress. Hidden away in remote mountains, this rare species of diminutive train would be surprisingly successful at avoiding extinction, with narrow-gauge freight trains still fighting their way over Cumbres Pass as late as 1968.

ESCAPE FROM THE BLACK CANYON

In an effort to negotiate the terrain from Gunnison to Montrose, the Rio Grande followed the Gunnison River west. Soon, the river's canyon deepened. Had the railroad continued on this course, it would have lined the bottom of the deepest, narrowest part of the Black Canyon, now a national park. Cimarron Creek, a tributary of the Gunnison, provided an escape from this trap. The rails reached what would be the town of Cimarron in the summer of 1882. Steep grades over Cerro Summit to the west required that helper locomotives were added to trains, and Cimarron was chosen as the helper station, requiring engine-servicing facilities to be built there. In later years, Cimarron became a shipping point for livestock being moved to market or to winter range. The last train chugged through Cimarron in 1948.

Above, left: This unusually tiny rail-mounted crane is displayed at the Cimarron Visitor Center.

Above, right: As this train left the Black Canyon, the crew in this caboose knew they would soon be warming themselves over a meal at Cimarron—if this weren't a static display documenting a moment in history.

Below: Cimarron's substantial railroad facilities, pictured here in 1886, included a four-stall enginehouse and a water tank. (Courtesy, Denver Public Library, Western History Collection, X-11486. Photo by C. Goodman.)

Ten narrow-gauge locomotives, numbered from 480 to 489, were purchased by the Rio Grande in 1925 from the Baldwin Locomotive Works. One of those locomotives, numbered 482, awaits the call of duty to haul a Durango & Silverton train.

Rails to Silverton

Silverton is a mining camp, a jewel in a most unusual setting. It lies in a dimple of the San Juan Mountains called Bakers Park, a small, flat valley not quite at ten thousand feet. Gushing out the southeastern corner of Bakers Park is the Animas River, or Rio de las Animas Perdidas, the River of Lost Souls. After the discovery of rich silver deposits, it wasn't long before trains battled up the canyon of this river to tap the wealth of Silverton's mines. By the summer of 1882, you could hear the whistles of Rio Grande engines echoing across the mountain-rimmed valley. The rush was on. As in much of Colorado, railroads had no real competition. Huge and heavy, mining and milling machinery could only arrive by train, and concentrated ore left the same way. No one in their right mind would

spend days snowshoeing over the frigid mountaintops when Durango was only a few hours away in a heated narrow-gauge coach.

The 1893 Silver Panic badly wounded Silverton. Years of uncertainty followed. Some mines played out. Others reopened. More than once, flash floods roared down the Animas canyon, and the town's vital steel artery was severed. Almost imperceptibly, Silverton's economy declined. Highways, such as they were, arrived in town, and automobiles competed with the railroad. But still, the railroad chugged along. Three times a week, a mixed train (a train carrying both freight and passengers) would make the round trip from Durango. Sometimes, the sounds of a trainload of sheep could be heard as they were railroaded to the high country for summer grazing. There was an occasional car of coal destined for Silverton and always cars of concentrated ore for the return trip to Durango.

This little branch line might have died when the Sunnyside Mine closed in 1953, but something unexpected had happened following World War II. Passengers had started to fill the little trains. While a few extra seats in the caboose had once been sufficient for the locals, now an extra coach was needed—then a half dozen extra coaches—then a dozen coaches. At first, in the late 1940s, most visitors were railroad buffs, but it didn't take long before word of this special train ride spread. Tourism began a long steady increase in southwestern Colorado—a mirror image of the decline of mining. Starting in 1954, freight was hauled up the canyon only on an occasional freight train as needed. The Silverton branch had become a railroad whose business was primarily entertainment rather than transportation. Ridership increased so dramatically in the 1960s that the railroad was forced to build its first brand-new narrow-gauge passenger coaches since 1904! Still more passengers came. The locomotives struggled up the hill with as many as twelve coaches. That was not enough. Starting in 1963, two trains were run each day. A third train was added in 1982, and a fourth train to Silverton started polishing the rails in 1986. On some days, additional trains made shorter trips up the canyon. The combination of rugged mountain scenery, narrow-gauge steam locomotives, and an authentic historical experience was irresistible.

The "Silverton," as this antique train came to be known, escaped oblivion once again in 1970 when the flooding Animas River ate away six miles of track, and the Rio Grande decided to rebuild it. In 1991, the Sunnyside Mine closed, yet again, and Silverton now depended on its history for its economy. The Rio Grande abandoned the rest of its narrow-gauge empire in 1968 and sold the Silverton branch in 1981. The hundred-year-old tracks were rechristened the Durango & Silverton Narrow Gauge Railroad. Track and bridges were strengthened so larger locomotives could travel all the way to Silverton. More historic locomotives were restored to operation and more trains ran.

The train to Silverton rumbles over a bridge across the Animas River.

Above: *Hermosa is one of several water stops along the way from Durango to Silverton.*

Facing page: *Headed south through the great rock cut at Rockwood, this train has just traversed the High Line above the Animas River.*

Tragically, the historic Durango roundhouse burned in February 1989 with all of the narrow-gauge locomotives inside. A heartbroken and determined railroad repaired the locomotives and was able to run trains that very summer. Within a year, a new roundhouse again stabled the iron ponies. Sold once more in 1998, the Silverton still steams up the canyon of the Rio de las Animas Perdidas as one of the greatest living-history experiences in the world.

Exploring: The Durango & Silverton Narrow-Gauge Railroad

The Marshall Pass railroad grade is now an unpaved road between U.S. Highway 285 near the summit of Poncha Pass and the old railroad town of Sargents on U.S. Highway 50, west of the Monarch Pass summit. There are railroad structures still standing in Sargents. A narrow-gauge train, depot, and water tank

are displayed in the large, interesting Pioneer Museum on the east side of Gunnison. There is a caboose displayed at the Hinsdale County Museum in Lake City. Other mining camps you might visit include Creede and Crested Butte. The National Park Service has a museum, including railroad cars, at Cimarron. Drive a short road east from there to see a restored narrow-gauge train displayed on an original bridge. The railroad displays at Cimarron are part of the Curecanti National Recreation Area, where a summer boat tour sails over the submerged route of the Rio Grande in the Black Canyon. Don't miss riding the train between Durango and Silverton. Providing passenger service to Silverton since 1882, the Durango & Silverton provides a spectacular tour of great historical significance. You'll enjoy the railroad's two museums: one in the Silverton depot and another in the Durango roundhouse.

CHAPTER 11

A Quartet of Mountain Wonders

The Trains of the San Juan Range

As the Civil War ended, men released from service expected to find their fortunes in the American West. Among them was Russian immigrant Otto Mears. Starting in 1871, Mears built a network of toll roads in Colorado's San Juan Mountains to tap their newfound riches. As the rush to the San Juans gathered momentum, Mears's toll roads were gradually replaced by railroads. In some cases, the rails were laid right on top of his old grade. Progress wasn't lost on Mears, and he undertook the building of his own railroads, which laid track in places the Rio Grande feared to tread!

Rails over the Rainbow

In 1882 and 1883, Mears built a toll road from Silverton to Ouray, which tapped the Red Mountain Mining District. It was there that Mears decided to launch his railroad empire with a railroad that would crest at 11,113 feet. The Silverton Railroad, also known as the "Rainbow Route," proved to be the corkscrew that opened the bottle, allowing silver to flow downhill along the eighteen-mile narrow-gauge track. Corkscrews were to be a theme for the railroad.

The first corkscrew in the Rainbow Route's story was the "corkscrew turntable," which was built at the end of a switchback near the highest point of the railroad and protected by a shed from winter's fury. A turntable is a rotating bridge in a pit in the earth. Normally found in railroad yards, turntables rotate steam locomotives end for end. The corkscrew turntable was different. It was the only turntable ever built on the mainline of a railroad. With no room on the mountainside for any alternative, the turntable spun the little locomotives to traverse the

Facing page: Narrow-gauge locomotives once took water at the Trout Lake tank.

Inset: You can still see the remains of mines in the Red Mountain Mining District as you drive between Silverton and Ouray. Most of the mines served by the Rainbow Route were here, at eleven thousand feet above sea level.

7 percent grades safely and access the mines beyond. So unusual was this arrangement that it was the subject of an article in the *Transactions of the American Society of Civil Engineers*. Some Narrow-Gauge Circle excursions were routed over the Rainbow Route. It must have been frightening enough to bounce up Mears's toll road in the stagecoach from Ouray. Not knowing what was yet ahead, passengers were surely relieved to board the Rainbow Route's trains at Ironton. History does not record what eastern tourists said about the operation of the turntable, but it was surely a memorable experience. Part of the procedure required the passenger coaches to coast through the turntable onto the mountainside beyond to be halted

by a brakeman winding down the car's handbrake!

The second corkscrew was used in the Rainbow Route's diner to open champagne bottles. That's right—a diner. The "Animas Forks" was a narrow-gauge Pullman sleeping car on the Rainbow Route line. One end retained a few sleeping berths while the other was a diner that included a kitchen and a wine closet. Serving caviar to champagne, the elegant car received national publicity.

Mears was an expert at garnering publicity for his railroad and mining ventures. Railroad passes—small, printed cards entitling their holder to free transportation—were issued to anyone and everyone who might benefit a railroad. You must have been really

Otto Mears, "Pathfinder of the San Juans," proudly poses at the far left of this turn-of-the-twentieth-century photo of the first passenger train on his Rainbow Route. (Courtesy, Denver Public Library, Western History Collection, MCC-3222. Photo by C. Goodman.)

Passengers transfer from steam to horsepower at Red Mountain town to continue their trip to Ouray after the arrival of the Rainbow Route's first passenger train in September 1888. (Courtesy, Denver Public Library, Western History Collection, X-11522. Photo by C. Goodman.)

unimportant if you actually paid for a train ticket. Mears found a way to rise above this sea of paper railroad passes by issuing ones made of buckskin in 1888. Finding leather not very durable, he then issued passes made of silver, and even a few of gold. These precious-metal passes often included delicate filigree or took some unusual shape. As you might imagine, they were noticed by the lucky few who received them and provided the publicity that Mears needed.

The Rainbow Route was spectacularly success-ful. Hauling ore so rich that armed men guarded it on its way to the smelter, how could the railroad fail? Its tracks reached their farthest extent in 1889 when they arrived at Albany, but Mears was still busy building railroads. His Silverton Northern Railroad followed the Animas River to another astonishing

11,200-foot altitude. Although known for his tenacity, Mears found failure on the Silverton Northern's last four miles, which reached the town of Animas Forks in 1904. After negotiating a year-round contract to haul concentrated ore from a mill near the railroad's terminus, he was determined to keep the line open all winter. The railroad was to be covered with snow-sheds, and a five-hundred-foot-long shed was built to test the concept. Its titanic timbers splintered into kindling when hit by the first snow slide of the sea-son, and the year-round contract was not renewed. Steep grades, short trains, and snow removal did not prove as big a handicap to any of Mears's lines as it did elsewhere in Colorado, however. After all, his only competition was a steep walk or an animal-hauled wagon rather than another railway, and there was so

Trainloads of concentrated ore left the Silver Lake Mill, the largest source of traffic on the Silverton Northern. Here, the mill is pictured in the late 1800s. (Courtesy, Denver Public Library, Western History Collection, X-62275.)

Above: *As the Rio Grande Southern's antique trains circled Trout Lake, they rattled over this trestle.*

Left: *A Rio Grande Southern trestle still stands near Highway 62 on Dallas Divide, just west of Ridgway.*

Right: Coal once tumbled out of these chutes into the tenders of locomotives at Vance Junction, near Telluride.

Below: Here, at the summit of Lizard Head Pass, sheep were loaded into double-decked stock cars each fall for the trip to lower ranges.

A water tank is all that remains of the Rio Grande Southern's facilities at Rico, which also included large yards, an enginehouse, and a depot.

much wealth above Silverton that Mears could charge what he needed to keep his railroad operating.

Mears would buy the independently constructed Silverton, Gladstone & Northerly Railroad in 1915 and fold all three lines into a miniature railroad empire in this remote mountain valley. Although all three railroads totaled less than forty miles, they were essential to the economy of Silverton. Without Mears's railroads, much less wealth would have been taken from the mines and at much greater expense.

Mears stood at Ironton, at the end of the Rainbow Route, and gazed down his toll road—the route of today's Million Dollar Highway to Ouray. In his mind, he could hear the triumphant whistle of a locomotive as it pulled into Ouray from Silverton. An 1892 survey for the Ouray & Ironton Electric Railway, Light and Power Company proposed an electric railroad with 7 percent grades and a complete spiral of track on the outskirts of Ouray. Instead of bridging this rugged 8-mile gap, Mears would

build the 162-mile Rio Grande Southern. Travelers from Ironton to Ouray could ride the Rainbow Route to Silverton, the Rio Grande to Durango, the Rio Grande Southern to Ridgway, and another Rio Grande train to Ouray—a journey of over 235 miles. How many do you suppose chose the 8-mile stagecoach ride instead?

Rails over Lizard Head

By 1890, civilization had reached the Colorado Front Range. More than one railroad supplied Colorado's prosperous cities such as Denver, Colorado Springs, and Pueblo. In 1890, the first trolley provided public transit to the citizens of Colorado Springs. Rio Grande trains carried eastern visitors to Manitou Springs where, starting in 1891, they could climb 14,110-foot Pikes Peak by simply boarding the coaches of the Cog Railroad. Luxury hotels and fine restaurants catered to wealthy visitors and Cripple Creek millionaires alike. In stark contrast, luxuries had yet to arrive west of

This mine near Telluride once provided traffic to the Rio Grande Southern.

Durango. Wagons hauling supplies became mired in the mud on primitive roads to the mining towns of Telluride and Rico. Winters were rough, and men on snowshoes struggled through blizzards. It's no wonder that the Rio Grande Southern was welcomed to this western edge of the San Juan Mountains.

Otto Mears began construction in 1890. The 162-mile mainline of the Rio Grande Southern, as well as the 10-mile Telluride branch, were completed in 1891. The line served coal mines west of Durango and then circled around, first westbound through Mancos and then eastbound through Dolores, to reach the mining camp of Rico. Dolores was a center of logging activity, and a tangle of rails reached out into the woods. A geared steam locomotive would haul ore down the steep branch line draped over the mountainside east of Rico. The mainline continued northeast, climbing 10,222-foot Lizard Head Pass before descending past Trout Lake to reach Ophir, named after the biblical location of King Solomon's mines. At Vance Junction, the Telluride branch looped up the hillside. The main track headed west to Placerville where it changed direction yet again to continue east to cross Dallas Divide and arrive in Ridgway, its northern terminus and home to the railroad's main shops.

The Rio Grande Southern embodied the essence of Colorado railroading. Its narrow-gauge tracks, directly laid on mother earth, would be forever innocent of rock ballast. Like a drunkard, its line staggered back and forth through the mountains. Tiny locomotives challenged huge granite monoliths as they rattled over hundreds of timber trestles. The railroad would never have the money to fill the trestles with dirt. It would pay the expenses of maintaining them and, later, the consequences of not maintaining them until its last train ran. It owned almost fifty locomotives but all were purchased secondhand. Nevertheless, it was essential to the well-being of the population it served. Except at its ends, no competing railroad came close to the line.

On a railroad planted in the middle of breathtaking mountain grandeur, the Ophir Loop was a scenic highlight of the trip. Two levels of track climbed the mountain's wall at Ophir with a hairpin loop connecting them. Trestle after trestle perched on the heights of Ophir. On his first inspection trip, upon seeing the most precipitous trestle of the Ophir Loop, Otto Mears stopped his train, walked across the trestle and motioned the engineer to follow. He was not about to trust the spindly wooden supports high above the valley floor until they had proved themselves solid!

How could Albert Einstein, the greatest twentieth-century physicist, be connected to this antediluvian relic of the nineteenth century? Einstein's letter to President Franklin Roosevelt informing him of the feasibility of developing an atomic bomb prompted the search for uranium. The mines in Telluride had been discarding worthless uranium ore in their waste dumps for decades. During World War II, machine-gun-carrying federal agents rode Rio Grande Southern narrow-gauge steam trains filled with the uranium ore that was destined to be part of the world's first atomic bombs.

There would be little hope for a railroad that couldn't even pay its operating expenses. Starting in the 1930s, the Rio Grande Southern built a series of weird and wonderful gas-powered rail vehicles that came to be known as "Galloping Geese"—supposedly because their gait resembled the waddle of a goose. The Geese added two decades to the life of the railroad. A Goose required only one crew member instead of the four required on a steam train. Ore and livestock were still hauled behind tiny puffing dragons, but everything else would travel by Goose! Passengers, small parcels of freight, and the U.S. Mail all got around the mountains on these gasoline-guzzling birds.

Ashes to Ashes

Just as his little locomotives had scattered their ashes in the San Juans, Otto Mears's ashes were scattered there after his death in 1931. The Rainbow Route had been abandoned in 1922, but the track lay dormant in the mountains until removed in 1926. Although train whistles had not been heard along Cement Creek since 1924, the Silverton, Gladstone & Northerly rails lay on the ground for another dozen years, waiting for a train

Above and Right: Galloping Goose 5 waits outside the Dolores depot. This Goose has been restored and sometimes operates on the railroads at Durango or Chama. A short track at Delores allows for limited, infrequent operations. The replica depot houses a small but interesting museum.

that never came. Those difficult last four miles of the Silverton Northern were gone in 1936, while the rest of the railroad saw a very occasional train until abandonment in 1942. Nineteen forty-three saw the last of Otto Mears's locomotives hauled from their home in Silverton for the long journey to the White Pass & Yukon, where they would help win World War II.

The urgency of uranium mining ended with the surrender of Japan. With little traffic not already siphoned off by automobiles and trucks, the Rio Grande Southern tried advertising for tourists to ride the wild Geese. Timing is everything, however, and the great tourist bonanza that saved the Rio Grande's Silverton branch was still a decade away. Southwestern Colorado was still wild, remote, and unknown in the late 1940s. When the Rio Grande Southern expired in 1951, it had yet to pay a single dime in dividends to any stockholder, still owed the full amount of its construction debt from 1891, and owed an even larger amount of interest on that debt, unpaid since 1922. As the space age neared, the railroad's assets included over 172 miles of decrepit narrow-gauge track and a museum-load of antique railroad equipment that was old when first purchased!

Exploring: Mines Among the Rainbows

U.S. Highway 550 follows the Rainbow Route northwest from Silverton to Ironton with some great views of the mines served by the Silverton Railway. An unpaved road from Silverton follows the Silverton, Gladstone & Northerly up Cement Creek. Another unpaved road struggles up the Animas River to Animas Forks, passing a square water tank at Eureka. This road is on the Silverton Northern's railroad grade for the last few miles before Animas Forks, the section of railroad that defeated Otto Mears's attempts at all-weather operation. You'll also find a mine tour and the Mayflower Mill open for tours. The Silverton Northern engine house at 9th and Cement Streets in Silverton is the new home of restored Rio Grande locomotive 315.

Colorado Highways 62, 145, and 184 and U.S. Highway 160 roughly follow the Rio Grande Southern's path from Ridgway to Durango. A railroad museum at Ridgway includes a historically accurate reproduction of Goose Number 1. You can spot a trestle just to the south of Highway 62 near Dallas Divide. Highway 145 parallels the route of the Ophir Loop,

but the best view of the Loop is from near Ames on an unpaved road. Farther north along this same unpaved route, you can spy the remains of the Vance Junction coaling dock across the creek. The Telluride depot still stands, and an original Goose is displayed in downtown Telluride, once pronounced "To-Hell-You-Ride" by witty conductors. An unpaved road circumnavigates Trout Lake where you can view a water tank and trestle. Read the Forest Service display about the railroad at the summit of Lizard Head Pass. Another water tank stands at Rico, a generally interesting town to explore. An original Goose has been beautifully restored at Dolores and sits alongside a reconstruction of the Dolores depot, which houses a museum and gift shop.

PART V

HISTORY'S TREASURES

When scrapped in 1921, the Colorado Midland was the longest railroad to be abandoned in the United States to date. Its demise marked the beginning of national railroad retrenchment. The Colorado Central and South Park tracks were torn up in the 1930s and 1940s. The Rio Grande's narrow-gauge empire in southwestern Colorado began crumbling in the late 1940s when the line from Gunnison to Montrose was severed. Soon afterward, the legendary Rio Grande Southern became a memory, and trains no longer crested Lizard Head Pass.

Colorado's mountain railways were the lifeline of much of rural Colorado and couldn't be abandoned until adequate highways replaced them. However, by the 1930s, most railroads knew their narrow-gauge segments were doomed and ceased spending money on them. Thus, many antique locomotives and cars were still running in Colorado long after such items were melted down or burned for scrap in other places. Although much was lost, an amazing amount of Colorado's railroad heritage was preserved. Large caches of historic locomotives and cars grace the preserved railroads at Durango, Colorado, and Chama, New Mexico, and many historic structures still serve their original purposes along their mainlines. Other treasures of Colorado's railroad history can be enjoyed at the Colorado Railroad Museum in Golden and at other museums and libraries scattered throughout the state. Some railroad artifacts still stand in the mountains as well, left behind after the tracks were removed.

What does this mean to you? Above all, it means you can experience Colorado railroad history in addition to reading about it and enjoying old photographs. You can even ride the same railcars on the same track that carried nineteenth-century pioneers into the mountains. This part focuses on the Colorado Railroad Museum and the Cumbres & Toltec Scenic Railroad.

West of Lobato Trestle, this Cumbres & Toltec train just passed through a small group of structures that are actually a permanent movie set.

491

C & S

10606

Burlington
Route

KEEP
OFF

CHAPTER 12

The Best Little Collection in Colorado

The Colorado Railroad Museum

I have often wondered what Bob Richardson and Cornelius Hauck would have thought if, when they were children, somebody told them they would grow up to found one of the nation's great railroad museums. Bob began collecting artifacts of Colorado's great railroad era in 1949. Living in Alamosa, he was strategically situated to act as the northern and western edges of the Rio Grande's Narrow Gauge Circle were removed. He also had the opportunity to watch the last years of operation of the San Juan extension of the Rio Grande. With the help of Cornelius, Bob collected everything from musty records to rusty steam locomotives. Quite literally, the collection included tons of paper and steel.

That collection was moved to Golden, and in 1959, the Colorado Railroad Museum welcomed its first visitor. The growth of the museum has been nothing short of phenomenal. Corporate records, photographic images, and ten thousand books fill a new library building. Locomotives, railroad cars, and trolleys—over seventy items of rolling stock—adorn the grounds. A new roundhouse provides a place for volunteers to preserve and restore these treasures. The collection ranges from an 1871 narrow-gauge business car to 1955 standard-gauge, streamlined diesel locomotives. Indoor displays interpret Colorado railroad history, and a huge model railroad layout entertains all who visit.

Facing page: Rio Grande narrow-gauge locomotive 491 frames a 1944 Colorado & Southern standard-gauge wooden caboose. The wood caboose was soon replaced by the steel caboose, which was then replaced by the electronic train-end device. Now, the caboose is almost extinct except in museums and on preserved railways.

Inset: What adventures this car's passengers must have experienced the Colorado Midland's High Line over Hagerman Pass. In later years, it frequently saw service on wildflower excursions.

This private, nonprofit museum boasts one of the largest collections of indigenous rolling stock in the world. In Colorado, many artifacts traveled directly from working railroads to the museum as rail lines, overdue for oblivion, finally gave up the ghost. Fortunately, the wisdom and resources existed to save a great deal of history.

Exploring: Railroad Relics

The Colorado Railroad Museum is still in Golden. Although the locomotives and railroad cars are the obvious attraction, don't overlook the many display cases of old photos and records that chronicle Colorado's railroad history. The bookstore has an exceptional inventory of books on Colorado railroads for further reading. The Forney Museum in nearby Denver also houses a significant collection of railroad equipment.

The ubiquitous boxcar carried both concentrated ore from Silverton and grandma's Christmas present to Gunnison.

Above: *Rio Grande Southern locomotive 20 is owned by the Rocky Mountain Railroad Club, along with several other historical treasures on display at the Colorado Railroad Museum.*

Left: *Milk cans wait to be loaded onto a combination car, usually called a "combine." Such cars had two sections: one for baggage and one for passengers.*

Above: Streamlined Rio Grande diesel 5771, built in 1955, stands guard in front of Rio Grande Southern steam loco 20, which originally hauled passengers from Florence to Cripple Creek on the Gold Belt Line starting in 1899.

Facing page: In the early days of railroading, locomotives were proudly named and not just numbered. When it left its Philadelphia manufacturer in 1881, locomotive 346 was christened "Cumbres" after the mountain pass with which it was to struggle for years.

Rocky Mountain Railroad Club volunteers paint Rio Grande caboose 0578. The club was founded in 1938, pioneering the preservation of Colorado railroad history.

Left: After years of adventurous journeys in Colorado's mountains, this little Rio Grande pop car enjoys a quiet retirement.

Below: Work Goose 6 was used to help dismantle the Rio Grande Southern in 1952. It faces the only remaining Rio Grande standard-gauge steam locomotive on a section of three-rail track. This special track allowed standard-gauge and narrow-gauge locomotives to use the same routes.

CHAPTER 13

INDIANA JONES
AND THE NARROW GAUGE
The Cumbres & Toltec Scenic Railroad

Even if you have yet to ride the spectacular sixty-four-mile remnant of the Rio Grande's narrow-gauge San Juan mainline, you would probably recognize this railroad, now called the Cumbres & Toltec Scenic Railroad. Have you seen the movie *Indiana Jones and the Last Crusade?* Do you remember a young Indiana Jones fleeing from his foes on a circus train, facing down lions and alligators, and almost being skewered by a rhino horn? These train scenes were filmed on the Cumbres & Toltec, as were scenes from many other movies.

The Rio Grande's San Juan extension was begun in Alamosa in February 1880 and quickly arrived in Antonito, twenty-nine straight and level miles to the south. There the tracks would diverge. One line would head further south and eventually reach Santa Fe, New Mexico—as near to the Rio Grande's original target of Mexico City as it would ever strike. The other line would head west over the mountains; these rails reached Chama, New Mexico, in time to celebrate New Year's Eve of 1880. By 1882, passengers could spend thirty grueling hours traveling the narrow gauge from Denver to Silverton. The lucky among them, with enough money, could actually try to sleep in narrow-gauge Pullman cars as they lurched around mountain curves. Automobiles and paved roads were far in the future, and this railroad marathon must have looked like heaven compared to days of jolting over steep rocky roads in a stagecoach.

The crossing of Cumbres, a pass 10,015 feet high, was key to reaching the San Juan's riches. From Antonito, the trains climbed a steady 1.4 percent grade to the summit. To maintain this gradient, the railroad wiggled up and down every side canyon of the Los Pinos River. Two places, the Whiplash and Tanglefoot Curve, sported hairpin loops of track to reverse direction and continue the

Facing page: A Cumbres & Toltec train coasts downhill on its way to Chama, New Mexico.

Inset: Before mechanical refrigeration, perishable foods were carried in refrigerator cars insulated with sawdust and cooled with ice.

climb. The topography was not as gentle on the west side of Cumbres Pass, and the tracks descended a 4 percent grade into Chama.

After the precious metal boom subsided and west-bound loads of men, machinery, and supplies no longer descended from the town of Cumbres to Chama, eastbound loads of livestock and lumber began to ascend the pass. Chama itself contributed cattle, sheep, lumber, and even oil to this parade of products. The muscle to boost these loads up the steep eastbound grade to Cumbres also resided in Chama. Eastbound trains would be broken into two, three, or more sections in Chama's large railroad yard. Each of these sections would be powered up the hill by two or three locomotives. Reassembled into a single train at Cumbres, it would head downhill toward Antonito, led by one locomotive. This complex operation required that locomotives and crews be stationed in Chama—and that all the facilities for servicing steam locomotives be located in this small New Mexican village as well. They are still there!

If railroad traffic headed west in its youth and east in its middle age, it reversed direction yet again in old age and headed back toward Durango. In the 1950s, oil was discovered near Farmington, New Mexico, south of Durango. As luck would have it, a branch of the railroad had been built long ago to serve Farmington, and the creaky, old Rio Grande narrow-gauge steam trains provided the most economical means to transport oil pipe and drilling mud to this latest natural-resource boomlet. During the 1950s, daily processions of trains lugged pipe to Farmington—the longest trains in the railroad's history. As drilling and development gave way to routine oil production, however, railroad traffic declined. Operations, once measured in trains per day, became measured in trains per week, then trains per month, and finally in trains per year. The last narrow-gauge steam-powered freight train ran from Durango to Alamosa in 1968, long after such trains were considered museum pieces in most of the country. Almost a century's collection of railroad artifacts awaited their fate in the Alamosa yards, and the San Juan extension slumbered in the mountains.

Above: A train arrives at Chama from Antonito, passing the coal tipple and sand house. Sand is dried in the sand house and loaded into one of the domes on top of the locomotive's boiler. It trickles onto the track to keep the locomotive's wheels from slipping while climbing Cumbres Pass.

Facing page: Locomotive 497 is larger than most steam locomotives on the Cumbres & Toltec. It was converted to narrow gauge from a standard-gauge engine.

Save Something

Suddenly, the American West was in danger of losing a great treasure—a microcosm of all the western mountain railroads—not just a museum re-creation but the real thing. The National Park Service looked at acquiring the property, but it was the states of Colorado and New Mexico that stepped up to the plate and purchased sixty-four miles of track from Antonito to Chama, nine steam locomotives, 142 rail cars, build-

ings, tools, water tanks, and everything that made the railroad what it was and still is.

The states may have owned a railroad, but they had no one to run it. More importantly, the Rio Grande had waited patiently for two years for the preservation effort to be consummated. It was in a hurry to dispose of surplus narrow-gauge equipment and dismantle tracks that would never feel the weight of a locomotive again. In 1970, a long tradition of hard work by dedicated volunteers began. For a month and a half, volunteers wrestled with a ninety-year-old railroad track that had not been tended for two years or maintained with any enthusiasm for decades before that. On September 1, 1970, a standard-gauge Rio Grande diesel locomotive hauled the first of three shipments of narrow-gauge cars and locomotives from Alamosa to Antonito and pushed them onto the San Juan extension, a track that would now become the Cumbres & Toltec Scenic Railroad. A fire was built in one antique steam locomotive, and after a monumental struggle, that locomotive with some of its rolling museum reached Chama on September 6. That was an average speed of twelve miles per day!

Railroads gave important passenger trains names in addition to their numbers; the Rio Grande's train to Durango was called the "San Juan Express" when it made its last run in 1951. The Rio Grande continued to run special chartered passenger trains as late as October 1966. Charters were especially popular in the fall, when the golden aspens contrasted with deep blue mountain skies. The five-hundred-mile round

Above: The Chama yard provides an education in railroad technology. The hose below the couplers allows the engineer to control all the train's brakes. Before automatic air brakes, the engineer would whistle for brakes and brakemen would jump from moving car to moving car, turning a wheel on each to apply its brakes.

THE FRIENDS

The operating arrangement envisioned by the states of Colorado and New Mexico made no provision for maintaining railroad artifacts not needed for excursion operation. By 1980, a group of friends began an effort to stabilize and restore the buildings and rolling stock not otherwise cared for. In 1988, this effort became the Friends of the Cumbres & Toltec Scenic Railroad. By the end of the millennium, this volunteer organization was an important force in the preservation and, most recently, in the operation of the railroad. Members of the "Friends" restore buildings and rebuild railroad cars. The organization acquires historic property that has strayed from the railroad, like the narrow-gauge tank cars that have now been returned from Alaska. With members numbering in the thousands, the group runs work sessions at which tens of thousands of hours are donated in an effort to preserve, restore, and interpret the history of this unique railroad.

The red car behind this Cumbres & Toltec locomotive is an extra-fare parlor car.

trip from Alamosa to Silverton was leisurely enjoyed over three days. In October 1970, four years after the fire of the last Rio Grande excursion was extinguished, the first excursion on the Cumbres & Toltec chugged out of Chama. The Cumbres & Toltec continues to enchant its guests to this day.

A Unique Railroad

Why is the Cumbres & Toltec so special? There are many reasons that combine to re-create the real American West here on the border between Colorado and New Mexico.

The place names along the spectacular route bring back memories of the Old West and the Hispanic heritage so strong in Colorado and New Mexico. Antonito. The Whiplash. Big Horn. Toltec. Osier. Los Pinos. Cumbres. Lobato. Chama. As the trains climb the sidehills to gain elevation, long views of evergreen and aspen forests entertain the eye. Westbound travelers pop out of the Rock Tunnel to find themselves six hundred feet above the Los Pinos River at Toltec Gorge. Trains carefully crawl out onto the shelf of Windy Point to open the view of the valley leading down to Chama. This is mountain railroading.

The size of the Cumbres & Toltec adds to the line's appeal. Serving two cities linked by sixty-four miles of track, the railroad is long enough to give the traveler the sense that this is a real railroad—a railroad that once carried passengers that needed to get to the other end—a railroad that once carried products to market. The sheer number of historic artifacts would stock several museums with many to spare.

Most of the technology of steam railroading is also here. There are water tanks all along the line, indispensable to producing steam. A coal tipple stands ready to load locomotive tenders. A roundhouse is home to tired locomotives. Scales wait to weigh freight shipments. Oil-tank cars sit ready to fill their bellies with the black liquid. You can almost hear the cattle bellow, waiting in the pens for their ride on the train. Rotary snowplows guard against next winter's onslaught. Depots, section houses, and other buildings dot the long thin line of the railroad.

The authenticity of the Cumbres & Toltec is striking. These very locomotives once labored over Cumbres Pass. They sped passengers on the San Juan Express, whistling through the same route run today. The rituals of this railroad's operation are virtually identical to those of a century ago. Fires are lit in locomotives. Coal is loaded for fuel, water for steam, and sand for traction. Cars are switched in the yard to make up today's train, which needs two locomotives to struggle up the steep grade. Machinists and mechanics repair the antique railroad equipment, as did their ancestors. The conductor bellows "All aboard," and the sounds of whistles blowing and steam escaping fill your ears.

It's all here. There is no interpretive sign to tell you that water was once taken from a wooden tank instead of a fire hose, or that the coal tipple was once thirty miles away and not part of the preservation. You discover these things firsthand. The atmosphere is difficult to quantify, but it just feels like an old-time railroad. For all the above reasons and because of the authentic ambiance of the hamlets of Chama and Antonito, you feel like you are in the Wild West.

Exploring: Sky Blue and Aspen Gold

Put the Cumbres & Toltec on your list of railroads you must ride. There are a variety of trips, some of which do not include the entire railroad. If at all possible, book a trip over the entire line. This is truly a sixty-four-mile-long museum.

Above: Until 1963, these tank cars were loaded here in the Chama yard from a pipeline connecting with an oil field to the north. Narrow-gauge steam locomotives hauled the crude oil to a refinery in Alamosa.

Facing page: A locomotive negotiates the Chama wye, an arrangement of track that allows the locomotive to be turned end for end.

Gondola cars are made to carry bulk loads such as coal. Some gondolas in the Chama yard can dump their loads automatically and others, like these, have to be unloaded by shovel.

Above: *A Cumbres & Toltec passenger train departs Chama pulled by locomotive 497, one of a class of ten locomotives assembled in 1928 and 1930 in the Rio Grande's own shops. Portions of these monsters, including their boilers and tenders, were recycled from older standard-gauge locos.*

Left: *Locomotives still quench their thirst at the Sublette water plug. Much of the railroad is set in a sea of golden aspen in the autumn.*

Above: There are two Rio Grande rotary snowplows on the Cumbres & Toltec. This snowplow, OY, is the newest and is also the last narrow-gauge rotary snowplow built in the United States.

Right: In a ritual as old as railroads themselves, a fireman fills a locomotive tender with water at Cumbres.

Facing page: A tiny narrow-gauge boxcar sits next to loads of new crossties. The replacement of wooden ties is a never-ending task.

Above: In 1971, the first year of regular operations as the Cumbres & Toltec, few trips were made, and most locomotives sat amid the wildflowers in the yard.

Right: The setting around Windy Point is immense, and views from the train are equally expansive at many places along the line. This train will soon arrive at the summit of Cumbres.

RAILROAD DIRECTORY

Before you visit Colorado's railroads, obtain the latest schedules and fares by contacting them individually. The most popular railroads require reservations.

Chapter 1
Georgetown Loop Railroad
888-456-6777
www.georgetownlooprr.com
Trains board in Georgetown or Silver Plume.

Chapter 2
Leadville, Colorado & Southern Railroad
719-486-3936
www.leadville-train.com
Trains board in Leadville.

Chapter 3
Manitou & Pike's Peak Railway
719-685-5401
www.cograilway.com
Trains board in Manitou Springs.

Chapter 4
Cripple Creek & Victor Narrow Gauge Railroad
719-689-2640
www.cripplecreekrailroad.com
Trains board in Cripple Creek.

Chapter 6
Amtrak
www.amtrak.com
800-USA-RAIL
Trains board in Denver, Glenwood Springs,
Grand Junction, and other cities.

Chapter 8
Fort Collins Municipal Railway
www.fortnet.org/trolley
970-224-5372
Trolleys board in Fort Collins.

Platte Valley Trolley
303-458-6255
www.denvertrolley.org
Trolleys board in Denver.

Colorado Springs & Interurban Railway
www.coloradospringstrolleys.com
719-475-9508
Trolleys board in Colorado Springs.

Chapter 9
Canon City & Royal Gorge Railroad
888-RAILS-4U
www.royalgorgeroute.com
Trains board in Canon City.

Rio Grande Scenic Railroad
www.riograndescenicrailroad.com
877-726-7245
Trains board in La Veta and Alamosa.

Chapter 10
Durango & Silverton Narrow Gauge Railroad
888-872-4607
www.durangotrain.com
Trains board in Durango.

Denver & Rio Grande Railroad
www.denverandriograilroad.com
719-873-2003
Trains board in South Fork.

Chapter 12
Colorado Railroad Museum
800-365-6263
www.coloradorailroadmuseum.org
The museum is located in Golden.

Chapter 13
Cumbres & Toltec Scenic Railroad
888-CUMBRES
www.cumbrestoltec.com
Trains board in Antonito, Colorado,
and Chama, New Mexico.

BIBLIOGRAPHY

The books included in this list are my favorites and are interesting, enjoyable reading. Some titles are out of print, so you may need to visit a library, a used bookstore, or the Internet to find a copy.

General

Beebe, Lucius, and Charles Clegg. *Narrow Gauge in the Rockies*. Forest Park, Illinois: Heimburger House Publishing Company, 1993.
Covering all of Colorado's narrow-gauge mountain railroads, this classic book is a romantic treatment of Colorado's railroad history.

Beebe, Lucius, and Charles Clegg. *Rio Grande: Mainline of the Rockies*. Berkeley, California: Howell-North Books, 1962.
Despite the title, this book includes all Colorado's standard-gauge mountain railroads. Like Narrow Gauge in the Rockies, it is a romanticized account.

Ormes, Robert. *Tracking Ghost Railroads in Colorado*. Colorado Springs, Colorado: Green Light Press, 1992.
Numerous maps and a narrative that explains how to find what is left of Colorado's railroad history make this book essential for serious exploration of abandoned railroads.

Chapter 1

Abbott, Dan. *Stairway to the Stars: Colorado's Argentine Central Railway*. Fort Collins, Colorado: Centennial Publications, 1977.
This is the definitive book on the Argentine Central and includes an amazing number of photos of this remote railway.

Ferrell, Mallory Hope. *The Gilpin Gold Tram: Colorado's Unique Narrow-Gauge*. Forest Park, Illinois: Heimburger House Publishing Company, 1993.
This interesting book describes the two-foot gauge railroad network in the vicinity of Central City.

Griswold, P. R. "Bob"; Richard H. Kindig; Cynthia Trombly. *Georgetown and the Loop*. Denver, Colorado: Rocky Mountain Railroad Club, 1999.
This volume covers the Loop from its construction to its reconstruction. There are chapters on the Argentine Central and other historic sites in the area.

Hauck, Cornelius W. *Narrow Gauge to Central and Silver Plume*. Colorado Rail Annual Number Ten. Golden, Colorado: Colorado Railroad Museum, 1987.
This is an excellent history of the entire Colorado Central from its construction to its demise.

Chapter 2

Chappell, Gordon; Robert W. Richardson; Cornelius W. Hauck. *The South Park Line: A Concise History*. Colorado Rail Annual No. 12. Golden, Colorado: Colorado Railroad Museum, 1974.
This is a very well-written history of the South Park and is considerably shorter than Poor's book.

Osterwald, Doris B. *High Line to Leadville: A Mile by Mile Guide for the Leadville, Colorado & Southern Railroad*. Lakewood, Colorado: Western Guideways, Ltd., 1991.
Primarily a guide to the current railroad trip, the book includes the history of the Leadville, Colorado & Southern and predecessor operators on this route.

Poor, M. C. Denver, *South Park & Pacific*. Denver, Colorado: Rocky Mountain Railroad Club, 1976.
This is the classic work on the history of the South Park.

Chapter 3

Abbott, Morris W. *The Pike's Peak Cog Road*. Colorado Springs, Colorado: Pulpit Rock Press, 1993.
This book does a great job of covering the history of the Manitou & Pike's Peak from its beginnings to about 1972, its original publication date.

Chapter 4

Cafky, Morris. *Rails Around Gold Hill*. Denver, Colorado: Rocky Mountain Railroad Club, 1955.
This is the classic work on Cripple Creek's railroads.

McFarland, Edward M. "Mel." *The Cripple Creek Road: A Midland Terminal Guide and Data Book*. Boulder, Colorado: Pruett Publishing Company, 1984.
This book includes only one of Cripple Creek's three railroads.

Chapter 5

Cafky, Morris. *Colorado Midland*. Denver, Colorado: Rocky Mountain Railroad Club, 1965.
Cafky includes the history of the railroad, a complete physical description of the railroad and its route, and first person narratives of experiences on the Colorado Midland. This is an excellent book and is especially enjoyable reading.

McFarland, Edward M. "Mel." *A Colorado Midland Guide and Data Book*. Golden, Colorado: Colorado Railroad Museum, 1986.
This work includes a history of the Colorado Midland as well as information on its physical plant and route, both then and now.

Chapter 6

Bollinger, Edward T. *Rails That Climb: A Narrative History of the Moffat Road*. William C. Jones, ed. Golden, Colorado: Colorado Railroad Museum, 1995.
Including the complete history of the Moffat, this book is especially fun reading because of the first-person accounts of life in the American West along this railroad.

Griswold, P. R. "Bob." "The Emmanuel Story." *Denver and Salt Lake Railroad 1913–1926*, 181-190. Denver, Colorado: Rocky Mountain Railroad Club, 1996.
The indicated chapter is the history of chapel car Emmanuel's adventures on the Moffat.

Chapter 7

Bender Jr., Harry E. *Uintah Railway: The Gilsonite Route*. Forest Park, Illinois: Heimburger House Publishing Company, 1995.
This unique high-desert narrow gauge in far western Colorado included some of the largest narrow-gauge locomotives used in the United States.

Crossen, Forest. *The Switzerland Trail of America*. Fort Collins, Colorado: Robinson Press, Inc., 1978.
The little-known narrow-gauge Colorado & Northwestern traveled into the mountains west of Boulder.

McCoy, Dell, and Russ Collman. *The Crystal River Pictorial*. Denver, Colorado: Sundance Publications, Limited, 1993.
This interesting book chronicles the many short but unusual railroads in the Crystal River Valley.

McKenzie, William H. *Mountain to Mill*. Colorado Springs, Colorado: MAC Publishing, Inc., 1982.

Besides telling the history of the Colorado & Wyoming west of Trinidad, it includes the story of this railroad's operations at Pueblo and in Wyoming.

Chapter 8
Feitz, Leland. *Colorado Trolleys.* Colorado Springs, Colorado: Little London Press, 1975.
This short book includes a brief history of all of Colorado's trolleys.

Peyton, Ernest S., and Al Kilminster. "Last of the Birneys." Colorado Rail Annual No. 17, 230–279. Golden, Colorado: Colorado Railroad Museum, 1987.
This article presents the history of the Fort Collins Municipal Railway, including its restoration.

Chapter 9
Hauck, Cornelius W., and Robert W. Richardson, eds. "The Santa Fe's D&RG War No. 2." *The Collected Colorado Rail Annual, 41-47.* Golden, Colorado: Colorado Railroad Museum, 1974.
Despite its title, this article describes both the war for Raton Pass and for the Royal Gorge.

Le Massena, Robert A. "Tennessee Pass." Colorado Rail Annual No. 17, 124–229. Golden, Colorado: Colorado Railroad Museum, 1987.
This article describes the history of Tennessee Pass from initial narrow-gauge railroad construction until 1987.

Chapter 10
Borneman, Walter R.; Cornelius W. Hauck; Alexis McKinney; Duane Vandenbusche. *Narrow Gauge Byways in the San Juans.* Colorado Rail Annual No. 14. Golden, Colorado: Colorado Railroad Museum, 1979.
This issue includes the Creede and Lake City branches of the Rio Grande and an article on narrow-gauge private cars.

Chappell, Gordon, and Cornelius Hauck. *Narrow Gauge Transcontinental.* Colorado Rail Annual No. 8. Golden, Colorado: Colorado Railroad Museum, 1970.
The history of Marshall Pass and the Black Canyon lines of the Rio Grande are subjects of this issue.

Chappell, Gordon. "To Santa Fe by Narrow Gauge: the D&RG's 'Chili Line'." Colorado Rail Annual 1969, 3–47. Golden, Colorado: Colorado Railroad Museum, 1969.
This article tells the story of the rail line from Antonito, Colorado, to Santa Fe, New Mexico, the Rio Grande's closest approach to its goal of Mexico City.

Farewell, R.C.; Robert W. Richardson; John S. Walker Jr. "A Silverton Trilogy." *Coal, Cinders and Parlor Cars: A Century of Colorado Passenger Trains.* Colorado Rail Annual No. 19, 142–219. Golden, Colorado: Colorado Railroad Museum, 1991.
These three articles chronicle the history of the rail line from Durango to Silverton, including both the Rio Grande and the Durango & Silverton.

Osterwald, Doris B. *Cinders & Smoke: A Mile by Mile Guide for the Durango & Silverton Narrow Gauge Railroad.* Hugo, Colorado: Western Guideways, Ltd., 2001.
Primarily a guide to the current railroad trip, the book includes the history of the Durango & Silverton and its predecessor on this route, the Rio Grande.

Chapter 11
Ferrell, Mallory Hope. *Silver San Juan: The Rio Grande Southern Railroad.* Boulder, Colorado: Pruett Publishing Company, 1973.
This book tells the story of the Rio Grande Southern and includes one chapter on Mears's three little railroads from Silverton. The book looks longer than it is, as much of it is photos.

Sloane, Robert E., and Carl A. Skowronski. *The Rainbow Route: An Illustrated History of the Silverton Railroad, the Silverton Northern Railroad and the Silverton Gladstone and Northerly Railroad.* Russ Collman; Jackson C. Thode; F. Klinke, eds. Denver, Colorado: Sundance Publications, Limited, 1993.
This story of the three railroads that ran north of Silverton is beautifully done.

Chapter 12
Albi, Charles, and Cornelius W. Hauck. *Colorado Railroads and the Colorado Railroad Museum.* Golden, Colorado: Colorado Railroad Museum, 1997.
Including an all-too-brief section on the museum's own history, this booklet includes a short history of Colorado's railroads and a description of the museum's collection.

Chapter 13
Chappell, Gordon. "Farewell to Cumbres." Colorado Annual 1967. Golden, Colorado: Colorado Railroad Museum, 1967, 1–27.
This article describes the history of the line over Cumbres Pass from construction to abandonment by the Rio Grande.

Osterwald, Doris B. *Narrow Gauge to Cumbres: A Pictorial History of the Cumbres and Toltec Scenic Railroad.* Lakewood, Colorado: Western Guideways, 1972.

This book does an especially interesting job of describing the initial volunteer rescue efforts in the fall of 1970.

Osterwald, Doris B. *Ticket to Toltec: A Mile by Mile Guide for the Cumbres & Toltec Scenic Railroad.* Hugo, Colorado: Western Guideways, Ltd., 2001.
Still including an excellent guide to the current railroad trip, this second edition includes history, operations, movies made on the line, and much more.

Turner, Robert D. *The Thunder of Their Passing: A Tribute to the Denver & Rio Grande's Narrow Gauge and The Cumbres & Toltec Scenic Railroad.* Winlaw, British Columbia: Sono Nis Press, 2003.
This is the only substantial history of the Cumbres and Toltec including the Rio Grande's operations on the same track. It is informative, entertaining and beautiful.

Wilson, Spencer, and Vernon J. Glover. *The Cumbres & Toltec Scenic Railroad: The Historic Preservation Study.* Albuquerque, New Mexico: Friends of the Cumbres & Toltec Scenic Railroad d/b/a, Windy Point Press, 2001.
Originally published in 1980 by the University of New Mexico Press, this revised edition is the most complete book on the Cumbres & Toltec itself including history, route, and artifacts.

Periodicals
C&TS Dispatch. Alburquerque, New Mexico: Friends of the Cumbres & Toltec Scenic Railroad.
This newsletter is sent to members and includes current information about activities of the Friends.

The Colorado Time-Table. Niwot, Colorado: The Colorado Time-Table, LLC.
This newspaper about Colorado's railroads will keep you informed on current events and historical issues.

Iron Horse News. Golden, Colorado: Colorado Railroad Museum.
This newsletter is sent to members and includes current information about the museum and preserved railways.

Many clubs, including the Rocky Mountain Railroad Club and several chapters of the National Railway Historical Society, publish newsletters about Colorado railroads. Contact information for these groups is usually listed in *The Colorado Time-Table.* Club members preserve history, ride special railroad excursions, and hike abandoned mountain railroad grades.

INDEX

ABOUT THE AUTHOR

Like many young boys of the 1950s, Claude Wiatrowski enjoyed toy trains. Scale model trains caught his interest next, but three academic degrees—including a doctorate in electrical engineering—and a career in technology slowed his avocation until his first encounter with Colorado's railroads in 1971. He moved to Colorado in 1975, and has explored much of Colorado's mountainous terrain, searching for remnants of its once huge railroad network. His train-related travels have taken him as far as Wales to see the birthplace of narrow-gauge track, which became an important part of Colo-

rado railroading. Eventually, the railroad technology of the industrial revolution became more compelling than the electronic technology of the information revolution, and in the 1980s Dr. Wiatrowski's hobby gradually became his profession. He has since written or provided photos for several books on Colorado history and produces videos on historic railroads. His productions have won Telly and Teddy awards, and one was selected for the Library of Congress Local Legacies Program.